The Psychology of

The Human Experience

Dr. Milton Franklin

Copyright © 2019, Milton Franklin PhD
ISBN   9781627190206
The Psychology of The Human Experience
Milton Franklin, Author
Yolanda Franklin, Editor
Published by Vizcaya International Inc.

Table of Contents

The psychology of The Human Experience

DEDICATION

This book is dedicated to the young men and women currently engaged in the existential battle to free themselves of the oppressive control of their parents' childlike thinking and belief system. The International Center for Intellectual Development serves as a support mechanism for all of these young men and women around the world. The simple yet powerful statement being made by this writing is that the era of intimidation is over. The gathering of thinkers that this book represents is a process that makes no apologies for the ideas it advances, and it will stop at nothing to empower those who dare to think.

A recent trip to Costa Rica where the organization is involved in building secured progressive communities for thinkers and their families, got me in touch with a group of young men between the ages of 19 and 28 who had all been raised in evangelical homes but had outgrown the childish thinking of their parents and their pastors and so were delighted to encounter a program such as the one we offer in this booklet. I have no doubt that like them, there young people around the world in search of reason, sanity and compassion. The theological chains that imprison them may be of a different color but it is no less oppressive, and an opportunity to break away from the mindlessness of their respective dogmas is something they are anxious to embrace.

Around the world there are thinkers of all ages seeking a forum in which to practice intellectual honesty that is going where the evidence leads them as it relates to everything in their world. They too will find a welcoming home in this organization.

The psychology of The Human Experience

INTRODUCTION

The United States of America is now forced to come to terms with the reality that they have elected as leader, a petulant and malicious 5 year old, one that has the nation traumatized and increasingly bewildered as they learn more and more about the person that represents them before the world, namely Donald J Trump.

This gives pause to the rest of the world that has had its share of criminals and degenerates posing as leaders of countless countries since the dawn of civilization. Europe, Asia, Africa and Latin America are no strangers to despots and vicious criminals deciding on their fate, but America for all of its problems had not yet stooped that low. The impeachment hearings connected to their current president is now giving them a taste of the kind of vile elements masses around the world have had to endure at one time or another.

Careers are being ruined and politicians have now reduced themselves to laughing stocks as they hopelessly attempt to justify the aberrant behavior of one who is now their leader. But even as the ship goes down, it is able to cause untold damage.

Because of its proximity to the United States, Latin America has always suffered disproportionately at the hand of the United States Imperialist activities, and the behavior of a degenerate president with is band of crooks, makes their situation all the more perilous. The grip the Unites States hold on the region continues to be a source rancor, pain and division as the people of that region see their efforts to take control of their own affairs truncated by a vicious force determined to call the shots as they seek to keep the region impoverished and beholding to their imperial masters.

Making sense of this massive conundrum requires some effort. In our case we've chosen the route of science and evidence as the only means for staying above the insanity that today passes for normal.

Having been trained adequately in English and Spanish, I've made it a point to make my ideas available in both languages. For that reason alone, it was difficult for me to publish a book that celebrates humanity at a time when nearly all of Latin America is on fire with the masses rising up against the corporate class and the oligarchs to reduce the working class to slave like conditions. I felt a profound analysis as to how this situation came about was absolutely necessary for as much as it has been ignored the source of the problem is psychological in nature. But psychology cannot be exercised effectively without a deep understanding of history.

A tiny group of people sprinkled across the globe have come to possess nearly all of the world's resources and its wealth. How this was able to take place deserves some explaining. It was a massive and extremely effective manipulation game that culminated in impoverishing nearly all of the world's masses. It is hard to fathom the level of ignorance among the masses that made such manipulation possible primarily because everyone today walks around with an information machine, a tiny computer that carries all of the world's information. We abolished the monarchy for the most part after World War Two, even though some continue to hang on through the mercy of what has to be a rather backward citizenry. It is impossible to imagine any people anywhere on the planet accepting the notion that there are actually human beings inherently and intrinsically more valuable than themselves. It is simply abhorring.

So, we have 4 distinct groups that have somehow come together to rule over the 8 billion people that inhabit the planet, those are:

1- The Monarchies with their supposed rights from god.
2- The Oligarchs who control the world's finances.
3- The Kleptocrats pretending to politicians.
4- The Narcho Lords who control the politicians.

In this scenario the working men and women have very little prospects for advancing. Many are now taking to the streets to express their displeasure with the ruling class and to inform them that they fully aware of the manipulations to which they the people are subjected to, and of the games that are being played on them.

Owning a publishing company allows me to quickly produce a book that more adequately addresses the reality of our times. Publishers make it a point to invest in a large number of standard book numbers or ISBN. This number allows for the distribution and sale of whatever material that is published.

It took many years of study but we've now come to understand the root cause of the human problemática, one that is centuries old.

The attack we launch on the Patriarchy; for which we offer no apologies; also reflects what we refer to as the ultimate form of feminism. This is because it has never been clear how women who declare themselves to be feminists continue to support empty and harmful religious concepts invented by men, for the benefit of men. Simply put, even though we argue strongly for the liberation and the eventual empowerment of women, it is clear to us this goal cannot be achieved unless women first develop the strength and the confidence that empowerment demands.

In addition to the young men and women struggling to overcome the tyranny of their parents' religion, the group we seek to involve in this movement are women willing to take the extra step in ridding themselves of all vestiges of male dominance, psychologically and physically. These are the ultimate heroes, and the ones we celebrate above all else. With their work and commitment, the respect and adoration for women can be restored.

A large number of topics are covered in this booklet, this is primarily because it serves as an information guide and required reading for members and potential members of our organization, the International enter for Intellectual Development. The workshops and discussions are all on these topics, and being informed is a prerequisite for participation in these high-level conversations.

REDEFINING EVOLUTION

The discussion over evolution has been altered significantly over the pasts few years as scientific investigation and revelation provides us with more evidentiary information regarding our planet, its history, and the history of life on it, particularly animal life.

Through these investigations we've come to understand that our planet is part of a Universe whose age dates back to more than 13 billion years. Our own star, our Sun, did not come into existence until 7 billion years after that. The 8 planets that were later to become a fixture in its orbit, including our own, did not come into existence until 500 million years after the creation of our star, and the changes it has endured in the past 4.5 billion years is nothing short of remarkable.

Because of all of that evidentiary information thinking people no longer engage in the debate around human evolution, that discussion is left for the overly patient thinkers who chose to engage them. Instead the discussion today is around the evolution of the planet itself from a ball of fire for nearly 3 billion years, to having its surface nearly fully covered with water billions of years after. That is the discussion on evolution we are now engaged in.

The second form of evolution we're willing to engage in is that of the evolution of life on the planet, particularly mammalian life.

We've learned from scientists and scholars that the first form of animal life on the planet was manifested in the oceans that were formed several billion years after the earth's mantle achieved temperatures that could sustain life. These were the uni-cellular microscopic life forms from which all other animal forms on the planet were derived.

After several million years the first amphibious creatures emerged from the oceans to continue their development on dry land and from these eventually the first mammals were derived. Unfortunately for the egos of most humans these first mamma-lian life forms were insect eating creatures quite similar in size and appearance to our current day rodents or rats. We can there-fore leave aside the monkey debate to process the idea that our real ancestors were rodents. For those who experienced difficulty with the monkey debate it is quite obvious that the notion of the rodents will be unacceptable to them which essentially brings the conversation on this subject to a painful end.

That crude reality regarding our past; without regard to those who accept or reject it; has the capacity to make modern humans somewhat less arrogant.

Ardrey (1963) argues that the roots of human ancestry is steeped in violence, and he does so by quoting the South African anthropologist Raymond Dart's 1953 paper entitled *The Preda-tory Transition from Ape to Man* in making his case. Dart's study leads him to the conclusion that man's ancestors were killer apes and that their weapons of choice in those early days had been the antelope humorous bone. Ardrey (1963) stated that what Dart put forward in his piece was the simple thesis that Man had emerged from the anthropoid background for one reason only, and that is because he was a killer. Ardrey goes on to quote Dart as saying:

> Long ago, perhaps many millions of years ago, a line of
> killer apes branched off from the non-aggressive primate

background. For reasons of environmental necessity, the line adopted the predatory way. For reasons of predatory necessity, the line advanced. We learned to stand erect in the first place as a necessity of hunting life. We learned to run in our pursuit of game across the yellowing African savannah. Our hands freed from the mauling and the hauling, we had no further use for a snout; and so it retreated. And lacking fighting teeth and claws, we took recourse by necessity to the weapon (p. 29).

Through Ardrey (1963), Raymond Dart goes on to present his case that this weapon could be a rock, a stick or a heavy bone and that in either of these cases it would have meant the margin of survival for our ancestral killer, but he added that the use of the weapon represented new and multiplying demands on the nervous system for the coordination of muscle, touch and sight. This combination of factors, argued Dart, contributed to the creation of a larger brain, a necessary requirement for modern man. Since that period, argued Dart, man has become a slave to the weapon, in other words, the weapon had fathered man (p.29). Dart's theory reflects significantly on the horrors on Nazi Germany despite the fact that it avoids the concept of the mistreatment of children as a contributing factor to the horrors we've all become so familiar with.

Ardrey (1963) does not answer the question of whether violence is imprinted in the species' DNA but the hypothesis regarding the weapon comes close to making that particular point. If Dart is right and violence has been with the species since its genesis, then it may well be that only through emotional and intellectual growth taking place at a massive level, that we will be able to overcome our violent tendencies.

OUT OF AFRICA AND ACROSS THE GLOBE
THE STORY OF HUMAN MIGRATIONS

The great playwright Robert Ardrey wrote:

Not in innocence, and not in Asia was mankind born, the home of our fathers was that African highland reaching north from the Cape to the Lakes of the Nile. Here we came about – slowly, ever so slowly—on a sky-swept savannah glowing with menace. In neither bankruptcy nor bastardy did we face our long beginnings. Man's line is legitimate. Our ancestry is firmly rooted in the animal world, and to its subtle antique ways our hearts are still pledged. Children of all animal kind, we inherited many a social nicety as well as the predator's way. But most significant of all our gifts as things turned out, was the legacy bequeathed us by those killer apes, our immediate forebears. Even in the first long days of our beginnings we held in our hands the weapon, an instrument somewhat older than ourselves. Man is a fraction of the animal world. Our history is an afterthought, no more, tacked to an infinite calendar. We are not so unique as we should like to believe. And if man in a time of need seeks deeper knowledge concerning himself, then he must explore those animal horizons from which we have made our quick little march. (Ardrey 1963, p 9).

Throughout its 3.4 million years on this planet the species has sought answers as to its origins. Unfortunately, this noble and uplifting quest is often offset by skillful manipulators who though few in numbers, have been able to convince large swaths of the species to the answers they've concocted out of thin air. These bodacious manipulators produce answers where there are none, and are responsible for the diminished curiosity that humans are gifted with. In short, they've put an end to the natural curiosity displayed by the species, stunting the intellectual growth of the overwhelming majority of humans. This sad reality is not expected to change for many generations. Club Vizcaya International and its budding communities around the world welcome with open arms those who have resisted the tyranny of the religious majority. Here they'll find other open-minded scholars who chose growth and compassion as a way of life. There is no room for prejudice of any kind at Vizcaya communities. Peace harmony and productivity drives everything in these communities. According to Spencer Wells of the National Geographic genealogical project, when humans first ventured out of Africa about 60,000 years ago, they left genetic traces still visible today. By tracing the appearance and frequency of genetic markers in modern peoples, they created an image of when and where ancient human beings moved around the world. These large migrations finally led the descendants of a small group of Africans to occupy even the farthest reaches of the Earth. Our species is African: Africa is where we first evolved and where we have spent most of our time on Earth. The first recognizable modern Homo sapiens fossils appear in the fossil record at Omo Kibish in Ethiopia, approximately 200,000 years ago. Although older fossils were to be located years later, this is our best understanding of when and where we originated from. The population expanded, and some intrepid explorers ventured beyond Africa. The first to colonize the land mass of Eurasia probably made it through the Strait of Bab-al-Mandab that separates Yemen from Djibouti. This first group spread rapidly along the coast to India, and reached South-east Asia and Australia 50,000 years ago. The first great incursion of our species beyond Africa had led us all over the world. Later, shortly after 50,000 years, a second group seems to have started an internal hike, leaving behind the certainties of life in the tropics to head towards the Middle East and southern Central Asia. They were ready to colonize the northern latitudes of Asia, Europe and beyond. About 20,000 years ago a small group of these Asian hunters headed for the frozen lands of the Arctic. With a storm on their face they made their incursions in East Asia. At that time, the large ice sheets that covered the far north had literally absorbed much of the moisture in its vast expanses of ice, reducing sea levels by more than 300 feet. This exhibited a land bridge that connected the Old World with the new one, uniting Asia to the Americas. When crossing it, the hunters had made the great final leap of the human journey. 15,000 years ago, they had penetrated the land south of the ice, and in 1,000 years they had reached the tip of South America. Some had even made the trip by sea. The story does not end there, of course. The boom in agriculture around 10,000 years ago - and the population explosion it created - has left a dramatic impact on the human genetic pool. The emergence of empires, the astonishing oceanic voyages of the Polynesians, identifies the Middle East as its entrance into the wider world. The so-called "multiregional theory", which contemplates Homo sapiens that intersect with archaic human species that already lived outside of Africa, is questioned by the finding that genetic variation in current populations decreases with Africa's greatest distance. The Middle East has a unique mix of African, Asian and European DNA markers, which indicates that the ancestors of all non-Africans passed that way. The Horn of Africa also offers clues about how our species could have spread rapidly along the coasts of Arabia, India, Southeast Asia and all the way to Australia. Sites with landfills filled with clams and oyster shells reveal that local people were familiar with coastal life and the exploitation of the sea long before any Red Sea cruise. Australia archaeological evidence for the remarkably rapid passage of modern humans to Australia, perhaps only a few millennia after leaving Africa, is supported by a genetic analysis that links Australian aborigines to that first wave of migration. They should have improved their navigation skills on the road, because getting from Asia to the continental land mass of which Australia was then a part would have meant navigating through a series of straits. Australia shared its prehistoric continent with what is now New Guinea, explaining why, genetically, at least, the island's indigenous population shares genetic markers with Australian aborigines. The two land masses lost contact due to the rise in sea level just 8,000 years ago. But while this glacial period allowed the first Australians to walk most of the way without getting their feet wet, their impact in Europe was much less welcoming. The first occupants of Europe did not appear until about 40,000 years ago. The genetic evidence points to Europeans who originated from a second wave of migration from Africa that took a tortuous path via the Middle East to the steppes of central Asia before leaning to the west. The challenges faced by these frozen pioneers are illustrated by the colonization of part of Great Britain. The first settlers of Great Britain were quickly dislodged by the fluctuating chills of northern Europe about 25,000 years ago. Evidence of a more permanent occupation is not found until about 12,000 years ago, when the retreating ice sheet and the warmer conditions tempted the refugee tribes in continental Europe, one in the southwest and one in the southeastern part of the continent. The sea levels remained low enough for these hunter-gatherers to make the trip by land, attracted by herds of and wild horses that had already made the crossing. Today, genetic patterns in European populations still retain traces of the time when their ancestors invaded the last ice age in southern shelters. The fossil record locates human origins in Africa, but science continues to search for details about the incredible journey that took Homo sapiens to the ends of the Earth. How did each of us end where we are? Why do we have a great variety of colors and characteristics? These questions are even more remarkable in light of the genetic evidence that we all descend from a common African ancestor who lived only 140,000 years ago. Through the eons of time, the whole story remains clearly written in our genes. When DNA is transmitted from one generation to the next, most of it is recombined by the processes that give each of us our individuality. But some parts of the DNA chain remain largely intact through the generations, altered only occasionally by random mutations, which become what are called genetic markers. The order in which these markers occur allows geneticists to track our timeline.

In the past few years scientist have given new meaning to the term out of Africa for even though it has been revealed for decades that Africa is the cradle of human kind and the birthplace of civilization, details on how the species migrated from there to the rest of the globe were not yet available.

The recent human genealogical project sponsored by National Geographic has already began to remove the mystery on how this development took place.

The study began and continues to be centered on an effort to trace mitochondrial DNA, the type of DNA that is traced only to the female of the species. This information is useful in giving the individuals a profile of their genealogical structures and helping them to predict some of the diseases they might be exposed to given their genealogical profiles. To get the job done they were compelled to produce a map of the migrations the species embarked on as they settled different territories around the globe. The deeply scientific complexities involved in DNA tracing is not something we are prepared to embark on in this manual but it is freely available to anyone who wish to educate themselves on this issue.

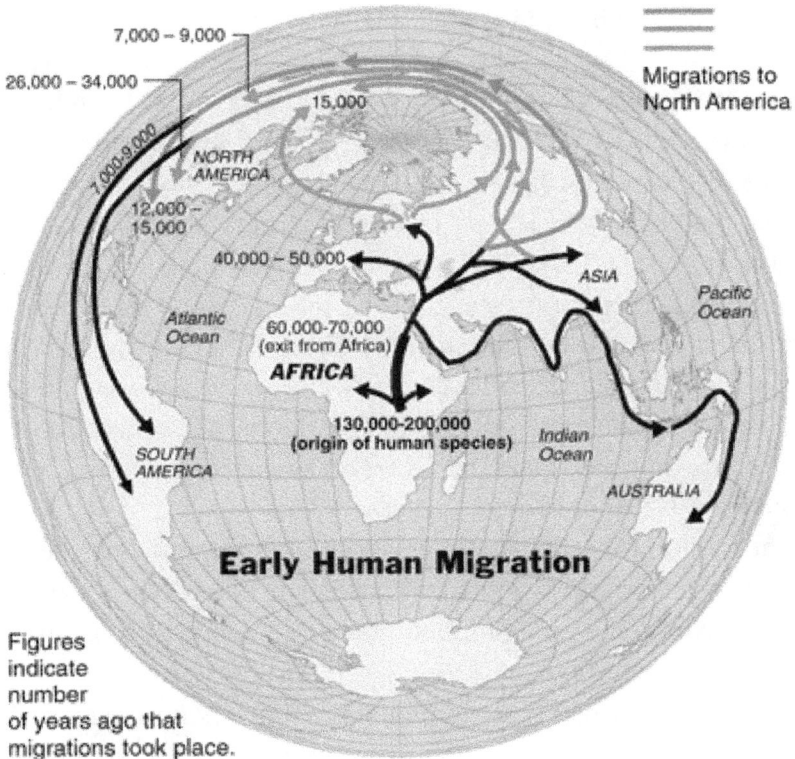

7,000 – 9,000

26,000 – 34,000

15,000

Migrations to
North America

7,000-9,000

NORTH
AMERICA

12,000 –
15,000

40,000 – 50,000

ASIA

Pacific
Ocean

Atlantic
Ocean

60,000-70,000
(exit from Africa)

AFRICA

130,000-200,000
(origin of human species)

Indian
Ocean

SOUTH
AMERICA

AUSTRALIA

Early Human Migration

Figures
indicate
number
of years ago that
migrations took place.

THE CONCEPT OF RACE

In his 1964 publication: *Man and his Ancestry,* Alan Houghton Broadrick stated: "The fact is that the word race should be left to the *racist* and not used in speaking or writing about anthropological matters. There is only one race, and that is the human race." (p. 31).

This statement epitomizes everything we attempt to do at the Center for Intellectual Development. We add to this the fact that race is a social construct, an invention if you will, by those who traditionally play the role of divide and conquer. They succeed at this by confusing the issue and by confusing everyone within their purview. Confuse in order to weaken. We've declared therefore that the term race for defining different groups within the human family is dead. The more enlightened members of the species have taken a stance against the manipulation and division that this term represents

Africa as the birthplace of the human species is no longer a statement that is in dispute within the enlightened members of academia. The current dialogue is around migration, and the process through which geographic location affected skin tone, facial features and other physical characteristics.

In the United States for example, the people of African descent have now come to proudly identify themselves as African Americans. That is a major step from the early XX century when Negro, and Colored were the words of choice for self-description. They were often put down with more derogatory terms but that will not be a part of the conversation in this booklet. Having renounced color for defining themselves is what is needed for this group to take that strategy one step further by defining the other groups in similar technical terms. In doing so, they will come to the conclusion that there are no white people, no more than there are yellow people, or red people. Because of its historic implications, the term white has come to symbolize superiority. Remove the term and the psychological playing field is leveled even further. What they refer to as white people are simply European Americans who arrived in America from various parts of Europe with a traditional aggressiveness that continues to characterize their behavior. It is imperative also, for the purpose of empowerment that they take the time out to study the psyche and the behavior of those they refer to as European Americans. This will instantly reduce the influence this group has held over them since the Atlantic slave trade. It will also allow this terribly oppressed group to begin forging a new world, one that is free from the undue influence. There is no doubt that the internalization of the scientific reality described here will help that process.

It is regrettable that there are so few African American of all ages capable of freeing themselves from the grips of Christianity and other invented religions. It is almost as if this people is intended to be in some form of slavery in perpetuity. In most cases the idea of living without their Jesus is unbearable, and you dare not insinuate to them that their Jesus was made up out of thin air by Hellenistic or Greek Jews.

To be ignorant of the history of the species leads to one thing and to one thing only, racism. For if we ignore the fact that the species is of one stock, then it is easier to presume that different groups are of different origins, and that some origins are superior to others. That is precisely the stuff that racism is made of.

THE BIRTH OF PATRIARCHY

Gerda Lerner (1920-2013), is one of the few authors with the courage to take on the study of the history of the patriarchy, providing her readers with overwhelming evidence regarding the birth of this system that has brought so much damage to the species.

I refer to Lerner as a pure academician, that is, one who engages the subject only through writings but is unable to venture outside of the academic confines to engages the problem, or as in this case call for the end of patriarchy as we are venturing to do in this writing and with the organizations I happen to be leading. Despite a hard-fought doctorate and all the work involved in such academic accomplishment, I am still an activist at heart so this campaign for the abolition of the patriarchy is a responsibility I simply could not evade. Lerner (1986) state that men weren't always consider superior or dominant. She makes it clear that because of her fertility, and because of the role she plays in the continuation of the species most if not all of the deities worshipped by humans were of the female gender.

This was a reality in nearly all cultures up until the Bronze Age some 3400 years ago. Sometime after that a group of people with an expressed hegemony on god, decided to invent one, give it male qualities, make that the god for all people and declared themselves to be the chosen people of that newly invented god. The new god became codified when the Roman Empire decided to adopt the Hebrew version of god, and to impose this infantile concept on the rest of the world. Today anyone who challenges that version of god is considered atheist, and there are people the

18

world over with the temerity to parrot a notion the Hebrews invented for themselves which is that they are the chosen ones of
that god who they invented.

Not only did the Hebrews invent their own god the also created a mythical figure and named him Abraham, their Patriarch.
To date there is absolutely no proof of the existence of an Abraham what he looked like and what family tree he is connected to.
A little over 200 years after this event a famine drove these people into Egypt for refuge and survival, and that they were there
for another few hundred years. The story of their exit from Egypt
is another tale that shrouded in mystery as there is no evidence of
a mass exodus or parting of the red sea by the god of their creation.

Not only is there no evidence of a mass exodus but its very
leader Moses, also turns out to be another mythical figure. As in
the case of Abraham, there is absolutely no evidence of an historic Moses leading the Hebrew people out of Egypt, but the
search cOntinues 4000 years on.

Sometime around 2000 years after this supposed mass exit a
group of Hellenistic Jew or Jews in Greece conjured up the story
of the god visiting earth 4000 years after he created it to take on
a 13-year-old girl and make her pregnant with his only son. Interestingly however, that story was not bought by the Hebrew
people in the rest of the Middle East. These Hellenic Jews named
their mythical figure Jesus or Josephus, and he was nicknamed
The Christ. To date, evidence of this Christ is nowhere to be
found but the story was persuasive enough for the creation of a
new religion.

So, we have a mythological god, with a mythological patriarch, followed by a mythological leader who led them out of slavery in Egypt, and finally a savior of the world that the Hebrew themselves want no part of. The point is all of these mythological figures add up to one thing, a massive manipulation to profess the superiority of the male figure by way of a male god and various patriarchic figures functioning as his staunch defenders. To this invented god they'll gladly surrender their precious lives, and they will happily murder anyone who does not submit to this creature of their imagination

With an understanding of this fairy tale and its chronology no one should have to feel guilty over not buying into the story that was invented for their manipulation. God and religion are simply human inventions and we're all just fortunate to be part of this experience called life. End of story.

As we contemplate the story of invention of gods and religions starting with the Hebrews, we can understand why to date there are upwards of 2500 gods and more than 4500 religions imposed on the species since we learned to communicate effectively with each other.

In the absence of any evidence regarding the natural world, the existence of a Universe or even the reality of their immediate surroundings, inventing gods and conjuring up religions was a very common occupation among humans throughout the globe. The one unfortunate thing about this practice is that as the species was dissuaded from the worshipping of goddesses and the idolizing of the female element, inventing gods and creating new religions took on a more sinister tone as manipulators found in this practice the easiest way to avail themselves of women's bodies.

The stupefying of women made it easy to convince them that they, the manipulators, were in direct contact with the god of their own creation and thus had a right to their allegiance and their bodies. The practice is so pervasive that even today as science reveals to us the wonders of the Universe, herds of women continue to pledge allegiance to the uneducated manipulators who claim to speak for the gods in their own minds, and there appear to be no end in sight for this practice.

In my childhood I was an open critic of the entire religious structure, and that is no less of a reality today. I recall a scene in Panama at the age of five after being sent to Sunday school with a group of cousins I was asked by my Uncle P (Percival Spencer) what did you learn from Sunday school Milton?. My immediate and instinctual response was: *Foolishness, pure foolishness*. It became a widespread joke among the extended family made up of aunts and uncles that had gathered in the home. He, more than anyone else realized that I was destined to be a rebel, or at least a nonconformist. The entire religious structure never made any sense to me, and since learning that they are all built out of mythology, that is someone's wild imagination, the case is even clearer.

I have to say however that despite my antipathy for religion and all of the silliness it preaches, it was only recently that I was able to make the connection between patriarchy and the invention of god. It does hurt that it should take me this long. There was just too much time and energy wasted. For too long I had to tolerate the idiots and their empty arguments without a properly formulated and satisfying response. But it is not too late, I've come across a group of young men and women who are desperately trying to break away from the silliness of their parents and they've found a home in the organization I created ***The International Center for Intellectual Development***. That is the definition of redemption.

We must be prepared for many more generations of this nonsense. Watching so called educated people of all races and ethnicities pledge allegiance to one of the thousands of gods confirms that reality that we're in this for the long haul.

With patriarchy came the male god and with it came racism, classism and silly wars.

EMPOWERING THE CHILD

No movement designed to address real problems and uplift the human family can be of any worth if it does not place the safety and security of the child before all else. The horrifying stories told by adults every day; women in particular; are glaring reminders of how we as a species have failed children everywhere. That, we insist, must change.

Franklin (2017) involves a detailed study of the organizations with a commitment to helping children and adolescents develop the skills for dealing more effectively with the insanity of their world in the hopes of becoming well-adjusted productive adults. It points to a missing element in all of these efforts. The first among these is the lack of evidentiary information about the world they inhabit. This is done in many cases to shield the child from the crude reality of the world surrounding them, but this strategy runs contrary to the strategy needed for the fortification of the child's mind and spirit.

In far too many cases the child is introduced to religion before him of her are able think, a habit that eventually stifles the child's intellect. This reduction in a child's thinking ability and reasoning capacity runs contrary to the aim at empowerment, leaving them with reduced defenses before the hate and vitriol that currently defines the world they're about to inherit.

Our organization the International Center for Intellectual Development is dedicated primarily to the safety of women and children, protecting them from the aggressive males in their environment whether this turns out to be a boyfriend, a husband a father or a brother. But we've learned that the task of protecting women and children is impossible if we do not remove from their subconscious the deeply engrained notion that men are superior and that they are the lowly vulnerable creatures subjected to the whims of those superior males.

The first order of training of course is psychological in nature, and most of it is composed of reality as it relates to themselves as members of a species that is still evolving. It helps them understand that the vitriol, ignorance and violence they witness is really a manifestation of the savage like state of this species that refers to itself as humans and that their own victimization is due entirely to that.

The second is much simpler, as it has everything to do with making the child physically strong, strong enough to detect, avoid and resist the aggression visited upon them by the more savage like adults they encounter.

It should be pointed out nevertheless, that the concept of empowerment is a relatively new one in our lexicon as traditionally, people never felt they had the right to be empowered. This concept was introduced in a massive scale by the young men and women leading the sixties movement as they demanded power for the people. A people that until that point had been completely powerless, and in nearly every sense continues to be just as powerless as they were a half a century ago. The question then continues to be: How do we go about empowering the powerless? A few thousand years ago some shrewd operators took on the mantle of Kings and Queens, and they somehow convinced the masses of the time, of their intrinsic superiority. This hypnotic control over the masses by an insignificant few lasted for thousands of years until the French revolution and others of its kind initiated a process in which that power would be arrested from those who claimed it for themselves. The process was bloody and untidy but eventually the masses came out on top. Some years later, we had some semblance of what was supposed to be a socialist revolution, one that was really designed to restore power to the masses. However, personality worship had already replaced the worshipping of the unseen and the unknown, giving individuals the opportunity to pose as gods, exercising the powers and privileges previously preserved for gods. That reality has lasted through our times albeit in different versions.

The revolt of any oppressed group grants the rest of the population an opportunity to crawl out from under their own oppression as someone else is taking their lives into their own hands by confronting power. What is real however, is that these revolutions bring with them some confusion and some lack of clarity that makes it possible for them to be co-opted and rerouted before their potential or intended objectives can be accomplished. There is a growing atheist movement and some feel this may actually be the long-awaited catalyst, but this group lacks the force and the passion to bring about any meaningful change. In addition, this group has not had to overcome oppression and discrimination brought on by their own natural identity. This book makes the claim that only an open challenge to the childish notions that drives all belief systems can really empower the masses freeing oppressed groups from the tyranny of the majority.

DECLARATION ON THE RIGHTS OF THE CHILD

From time to time, even those who labor for the protection of children need to be reminded that nearly a century ago the organization that preceded the United Nations established a strong and very clear declaration designed to protect the rights of all children everywhere. It is a public document so I'm taking the liberty to reproduce it here in this book designed to alter once and for all the relationship between minors and the world around them.

Declaration of the Rights of the Child, G.A. res. 1386 (XIV), 14 U.N. GAOR Supp. (No. 16) at 19, U.N. Doc. A/4354 (1959).

PREAMBLE

> Whereas the peoples of the United Nations have, in the Charter, reaffirmed their faith in fundamental human rights and in the dignity and worth of the human person, and have determined to promote social progress and better standards of life in larger freedom,
>
> Whereas the United Nations has, in the Universal Declaration of Human Rights, proclaimed that everyone is entitled to all the rights and freedoms set forth therein, without distinction of any kind, such as race, colour, sex, language, religion, political or other opinion, national or social origin, property, birth or other status,

Whereas the child, by reason of his physical and mental immaturity, needs special safeguards and care, including appropriate legal protection, before as well as after birth,

Whereas the need for such special safeguards has been stated in the Geneva Declaration of the Rights of the Child of 1924, and recognized in the Universal Declaration of Human Rights and in the statutes of specialized agencies and international organizations concerned with the welfare of children,

Whereas mankind owes to the child the best it has to give,

Now therefore,

The General Assembly

Proclaims this Declaration of the Rights of the Child to the end that he may have a happy childhood and enjoy for his own good and for the good of society the rights and freedoms herein set forth, and calls upon parents, upon men and women as individuals, and upon voluntary organizations, local authorities and national Governments to recognize these rights and strive for their observance by legislative and other measures progressively taken in accordance with the following principles:

Principle I

The child shall enjoy all the rights set forth in this Declaration. Every child, without any exception whatsoever, shall be entitled to these rights, without distinction or discrimination on account of race, colour, sex, language, religion, political or other opinion, national or social origin, property, birth or other status, whether of himself or of his family.

Principle 2

The child shall enjoy special protection, and shall be given opportunities and facilities, by law and by other means, to enable him to develop physically, mentally, morally, spiritually and socially in a healthy and normal manner and in conditions of freedom and dignity. In the enactment of laws for this purpose, the best interests of the child shall be the paramount consideration.

Principle 3

The child shall be entitled from his birth to a name and a nationality.

Principle 4

The child shall enjoy the benefits of social security. He shall be entitled to grow and develop in health; to this end, special care and protection shall be provided both

to him and to his mother, including adequate pre-natal
and post-natal care. The child shall have the right to adequate nutrition, housing, recreation and medical services.

Principle 5

The child who is physically, mentally or socially handi-
capped shall be given the special treatment, education
and care required by his particular condition.

Principle 6

The child, for the full and harmonious development of
his personality, needs love and understanding. He shall,
wherever possible, grow up in the care and under the responsibility of his parents, and, in any case, in an atmosphere of affection and of moral and material security; a
child of tender years shall not, save in exceptional circumstances, be separated from his mother. Society and
the public authorities shall have the duty to extend particular care to children without a family and to those
without adequate means of support. Payment of State
and other assistance towards the maintenance of children
of large families is desirable.

Principle 7

The child is entitled to receive education, which shall be
free and compulsory, at least in the elementary stages.

He shall be given an education which will promote his general culture and enable him, on a basis of equal opportunity, to develop his abilities, his individual judgment, and his sense of moral and social responsibility, and to become a useful member of society.

The best interests of the child shall be the guiding principle of those responsible for his education and guidance; that responsibility lies in the first place with his parents.

The child shall have full opportunity for play and recreation, which should be directed to the same purposes as education; society and the public authorities shall endeavor to promote the enjoyment of this right.

Principle 8

The child shall in all circumstances be among the first to receive protection and relief.

Principle 9

The child shall be protected against all forms of neglect, cruelty and exploitation. He shall not be the subject of traffic, in any form.

The child shall not be admitted to employment before an appropriate minimum age; he shall in no case be caused or permitted to engage in any occupation or employment which would prejudice his health or education, or interfere with his physical, mental or moral development.

Principle 10

The child shall be protected from practices which may foster racial, religious and any other form of discrimination. He shall be brought up in a spirit of understanding, tolerance, friendship among peoples, peace and universal brotherhood, and in full consciousness that his energy and talents should be devoted to the service of his fellow men.

It is regrettable that not all children can be protected from the abuse of misguided adults, some are in seclusion, held hostage by their parents or caretakers. But every child should know their rights. Every child should have a copy of the United Nations declaration on the rights of the child. The document should be read to them in class every day, and it should be discussed openly. The child should be encouraged to reveal when adults are not living up to their responsibilities established in the declaration.

A STUDY OF CHILDHOOD
JEAN JACQUE ROUSSEAU

In this chapter I will discuss some of the concepts and theories surrounding the issue of child development, particularly those concepts that focus on the role of experience in learning, in childhood. The theorists that are profiled in this essay are: John Dewey, Maria Montessori, Lev Vygotsky, Jean Piaget, and Erik Erikson. The views of these noted theorists will be compared and contrasted with that of one who preceded them all by more than a century, Jean Jacques Rousseau (1712-1782). I will attempt to explore whether any of these theorists derived any of their ideas from Rousseau or if they departed completely from Rousseau's thoughts.

Rousseau was chosen for a number of reasons, but chief among them is his unwavering commitment to the safety and security of children; at least as manifested through his writings. The controversies, and contradictions surrounding Rousseau's life also makes him a compelling figure for study and analysis for many scholars wishing to develop some understanding of or learn from the life of this enigmatic historic figure. Perhaps the most noted contradictions in Rousseau's life is his abandonment of his five children; none of multiple birth; to a foundling institution never to see them again. Scholars must make extraordinary to understand or explain away these and other controversial aspects of Rousseau's life.

Rousseau is considered by many to be one of the first successful novelists, having rendered his opinions on children through

32

two famous novels: *Emile* and *The New Heloise*. Rousseau presents the ideas for his character Emile through a series of five books which have come to represent five of the stages of his character's life, and although, like Rousseau, the other thinkers and theorists dealt with in this report, all subscribe to the concept of stages in a child's development, this report will focus on the complexities involved in the adult child relationship described by Rousseau.

At a time when the concept of the child was not yet defined, Rousseau endowed the child, and particularly the infant, with almost magical powers in their ability to command the attention of those around them, and the enormous care that had to be invested in securing its safety. We find in Rousseau (1979):

> At birth the child cries; his earliest infancy is spent in crying. Sometimes he is tossed, he is petted, to appease him; sometimes he is threatened, beaten, to make him keep quiet. We either do as he pleases or else, we exact from him what pleases us; we either submit to his whims, or make him submit to ours. There is no middle course, he must either give or receive orders. Thus, his first ideas are of absolute rule, and of slavery. Before he knows how to speak he commands; before he is able to act, he obeys; and sometimes he is punished before he knows what his faults are, or rather; before he is capable of committing them. Thus, do we pour into his young heart the passions that are later imputed to nature; and after having taken pains to make him wicked, we complain of finding him wicked (p.21).

Profound in its scope this analysis gives us as clear a picture of any other of the complexities embodied in the infant child and the struggles of adults to relate adequately to this creature, they themselves grew out of a few years earlier. This highly analytical and deeply psychological statement was made more than a century before the birth of the discipline we have come to know as psychology.

The dilemma that lies in reducing the powers the child holds, contrasted with the willingness or lack thereof on the part of adults to set this child free and allow it to grow unencumbered is one that will be dealt with in this book. In short, more liberty and less power, since the child neither requests nor has any need for the powers we attribute to it and it certainly is not happy when the other side of that power is applied to him or her in the form of punishment or other corrective measures.

It is this dilemma that will be explored here as we assess the approach of other thinkers and theorists to this most complex of subjects.

With some degree of accuracy, it could be said that this unresolved dilemma lies at the heart of much of the mistreatment meted out to children for all of recorded history, since in all that time as in the present, the specie struggled with devising efficient methods for raising children. That said, it can also be argued that Rousseau was one of the first to advocate for the safety and security of children, doing so without preceding theories or models that we know of. Thus, the striking of a balance between the freedom which the child yearns, and those magical powers attributed to it that it never asked for, will be explored in this book along with the opinions of others theorists and thinkers.

Mooney (2000) tells us that Dewey was born in Burlington Vermont on October 20th, 1859 into a farming family. He studied philosophy at the University of Vermont from where he graduated in 1879 with a degree in philosophy. Dewey went on to do graduate work at the John Hopkins University where he obtained a PhD in philosophy in 1884. After graduating, he accepted a teaching position at the University of Michigan. In 1894 he was offered a position at the University of Chicago that allowed him the opportunity to combine his teaching of philosophy, with two other disciplines: Psychology and Educational Theory. Mooney (2000) tells us that within 2 years he had established the famous laboratory school that attracted attention around the world. Dewey's Laboratory School established the University of Chicago as the center of thought on progressive education, the movement toward more democratic and child-centered education. Mooney (2000), tells us that Dewey's position at the head of the lab school was relatively short-lived but created, in a few years, a wealth of educational research and theory that continues do drive many of our best practices today (p.2).

In Dewey (1916) we find a rather sober reference to youth and our responsibility towards them when he argues that in directing the activities of the young, society determines its own future. The nature of the child will largely turn upon the direction children's activities were given at an earlier period. Dewey describes this cumulative of activities towards becoming a better person, as growth. (p.49) Dewey focuses on the powers children possess for enlisting the cooperative attention of others, which he claims is another way of saying that others are marvelously attentive to the needs of children. That they are egotistical and self-centered before adolescence is not lost on Dewey, but it is his conviction that even in their egotistical self-centeredness there are moments when they are able to capture everyone's heart. Stable adults recognize that this power the child possess for garnering their attention is only temporary, and even their egotistical self-centered behavior becomes more tolerable because again it is only temporary. The travesty Dewy argues, are those adults too absorbed in their own affairs to take any real interest in children's affairs (p.52).

Mooney (2000) presents John Dewey's *Pedagogue Creed,* published in 1897. In its first and second articles Dewey makes reference to the power of children. He says "True education comes through the stimulation of the child's powers …The child's own instincts and powers furnish the material and give the starting point for all education" (p.4). Here Dewey speaks, not so much of the powers of the infant but of with the potential powers of the child in the learning process.

In what might be one of John Dewey's most significant statements we have in Dewey (1916), "From a social standpoint, dependence denotes a power rather than a weakness" (p. 52), for it involves interdependence, and a child's gift for social interaction, coupled with its dependency all tend to facilitate social responsiveness and social interaction. Rather than being in awe with a child and its immaturity, surreptitiously granting the child all of that unrequested power, Dewey (1916) argues that respect for immaturity can actually work as a perfect antidote for all that power we give to the child and the resentment that naturally accompanies it, for it is in the resentment that the attitude towards the child changes thus placing them in danger. Evoking the words of Emerson, Dewey (1916) implores us to respect the child, its space its right to solitude, for in the end respect for the child invariably translates to respect for self (p.62). But returning to the subject of freedom Dewey (1916) reminds us that the important thing to bear in mind is that it involves a mental attitude rather than an external constraint of movement, but also that this quality or state of mind cannot be achieved without a freedom of movement that allows one to explore, to experiment, and to apply all that has been learned. Applied to the child, this concept may allow us to envision a healthier society, one with less cases of depression, or aggression.

Mooney (2000) then introduces us to Maria Montessori, the Italian physician, and education reformer. Although she argued for educational structure, Montessori shared Rousseau's views that freedom and play constitute essential components in a child's development, and that it is in these unstructured activities that much of their learning takes place. That it is in this natural unencumbered environment that the child gathers most of their valuable experiences. Like Dewey, Montessori attempted to bring about changes in the system of education, not only in her own Italy but also to anyone around the world willing to adopt her method.

Montessori subscribed to a more structured learning environment, one in which children begin formal learning at a very early age. In that she differs from Rousseau, but in ascribing more freedom and less powers to the child there was hardly any difference between them. In Kramer (1976) Montessori argue that freedom within carefully placed limits, and not authoritarian discipline, is the principle of education (p.7), and that is significant because the charges leveled at Rousseau by his critics is that he is willing to let children do as they please without any adult oversight or guidance. That overly simplistic approach to Rousseau on the part of his critics is effectively countered by Montessori when she suggests that this freedom ought to have carefully placed limits.

In Montessori (1912) we find a definition of freedom not as an external sign of liberty but as a means of education, and an overwhelming endorsement of Rousseau's views as it relates to the importance of adults respecting the child's freedom. Montessori describes the children in her school as the promise of things to come, and as the future of the specie: "They are the earnest of a humanity grown in the culture of beauty---the infancy of an all-conquering humanity, since they are intelligent and patient observers of their environment, and possess in the form of intellectual liberty the power of spontaneous reasoning" (p.84, 308).

Although the focus of this book is less power and more freedom, it is important to note that this does not preclude the natural powers the child possesses, not the ones given artificially to the child through misguided adults, powers they often remove at will, rendering the child in a lower position than powerless, it renders the child a victim. It is this natural power that is worth protecting. One such form of power, in Montessori's opinion, is the joy the child experiences when exposed to new knowledge. It includes the power to learn from the environment by means of the senses. In Montessori's opinion these are important forms of power (p.301).

In a direct reference to Rousseau and the similarities between them particularly on the subject of freedom and liberty for the child:

> The school must allow freedom for the development of the activity of the child; if scientific education is to come into being...No one would dare to assert that such a principle already exists in teaching or in the school. It is quite true that certain pedagogues like Rousseau set out fantastic principles and vague aspirations of liberty for the child, but the true conception of liberty is, in fact, unknown to the pedagogues (p.7).

The similarities between Montessori and Rousseau on the question of less power and more freedom is clearly established in their writings and perhaps in the writings of most thoughtful thinkers who have argued for educational reform.

The Swiss theorist Jean Piaget rarely addressed the issue of freedom and power as it relates to the child but we do find in Mooney (2000) references to the similarities that exists between Piaget and Rousseau on the subject of more freedom for the child to play and learn as much as possible through that activity as she argues that Piaget stressed the importance of play as an important avenue for learning. Mooney (2002) also added, "It is largely the influence of Piaget, building on Montessori's work, that encourages uninterrupted periods of play in early childhood classrooms. When children are interested and much involved in a subject, they need teachers who respect this absorption with their work" (p. 62, 73).

In an interview with Jean-Claude Bringuier, author of the noted *Conversations with Jempwerigean Piaget,* Piaget argued that in the history of science and the formation of man's mind, determinism has played too much of a role, that there have been too few crossroads and too little by way of freedom. (p.102) But in Muller (2008) we find a statement from Rousseau that appears to run contrary to the concept of freedom expressed earlier by Piaget, "Social transmission failed to explain why an individual may criticize collective beliefs in the name of human rights and truth, thereby contrasting the universal to the collective, i.e., truth to opinion "(p 12).

There are further contradictions emanating from Piaget in Muller (2008), when he tells us that according to Piaget the child first creates pretend play autonomously, through individual rather than social processes and through interaction with the environment rather than with people. This contrasts with the Vygotsky modeled soviet school that considers play to be essential (p.86).

The extended period for play which Piaget recommends, is the equivalent of Rousseau's concept of more freedom and both Rousseau and Piaget see play as an important part of the learning process. Piaget found no need to deal with the concept of power, concerning the child, because all of his time was spent observing them carefully, starting with his very own. This sharp and acute observation of children, along with his habit of engaging them verbally gave Piaget a special understanding of how they think and behave, thus removing from the equation the element of awe or the habit of conferring unrealistic powers to the child that are neither useful or requested.

Lev Vygotsky's work with children was not unlike that of Piaget as he too spent a great deal of time observing them and recording his observations. It is these observations that culminated in the theory he was able to put together, his noted theories on the subject of child development. The initial similarity Vygotsky holds with Rousseau lies in his embrace of children's freedom for endless play convinced that in play much learning takes play. Vygotsky rarely uses the word freedom but his emphasis on play and its importance inevitably invokes freedom since all play requires a level of individual freedom. Proposing the principle that children learn as much or more from the environment and from each other as they do from books or the curriculum, Vygotsky propose that children should have the freedom to create their own learning by choosing from the curriculum and from various classroom activities, the ones that best suit their needs and abilities. No doubt this level of freedom poses tremendous problems for teachers primarily because of class size and the challenge of evaluating the child's intellectual growth. That level of freedom proposed by Vygotsky must be matched with measurable results since when all is said and done, a child in the school system is expected to learn how to read, perform basic math and arithmetic, and conduct some basic reasoning.

We are told in Mooney (2000), that Vygotsky studied and responded to the works Sigmund Freud, Jean Piaget and Maria Montessori during their lifetime, and that he was greatly influenced by them, and that after graduating from Moscow University Vygotsky became a high school teacher, where his interaction with children and his careful observation of their learning peaked Vygotsky interest in the psychological aspect of the learn-ing process. This careful observation of his own students in the learning process, lead Vygotsky to develop his first theory which he referred to as: The Zone of Proximal Development. Vygotsky described the Zone of Proximal Development as the area or dis-tance that exists between the most difficult task a child can per-form without the assistance of an adult or more advanced student, and the most difficult task a child can perform with that assis-tance (Mooney 2000, p. 83, 89).

Although this report is centered on a comparative between Rousseau and these five theorists/thinkers, the parallel that ex-isted between Piaget and Vygotsky demands a closer look, and perhaps some more work by way of comparison.

Mooney (2000) tells us that Piaget was of the opinion that the child's egocentrism prevents it from perceiving the points of view of others thus making play less effective and more of a lone activity among these children. Vygotsky on the other hand, em-braced the value of play as a valuable learning tool particularly when performed in a social setting (pp, 90, 91).

In addition to play and its relationship with freedom, knowledge and information also play a significant role in the de-velopment of individual freedom either for a child or an adult.

In a review of the interaction between the social world and cognitive development Lloyd and Fernyhough (1999), argue that scholars have long been interested in the relations between social factors and cognitive development. Lloyd and Fernyhough (1999), tell us that in his early work, Piaget [1923/1959] argued that children below the age of 7are unlikely to benefit from social interaction, given the egocentric nature of preoperational thought. That children are like scientists, working alone on the physical, logical, and mathematical material of their world in order to make sense of their reality (pp. 311,321). Lloyd and Fernyhough (1999), also tells us that Vygotsky on the other hand believed that development, a social process from birth onwards, is assisted by others (adults or peers) more competent in the skills and technologies available to the cultures, and that development is fostered by collaboration within the child's zone of proximal development. They insist that Vygotsky's theory is the clearest example of a contextual theory which says that individual development cannot be conceived outside of a social world, and that social world is simultaneously interpersonal, cultural and historical. In other words, from a Vygotsky perspective one cannot consider social interaction between peers and between adults and children without understanding the historically formed social context within which that interaction takes place. Children's cognitive development is thus not the product of simply biological maturation, nor of interaction between them and others in their environment (pp. 311, 329).

The other term Vygotsky introduces is Scaffolding describing it as the assistance a child receives in his efforts to accomplish a particular task. We learn that the inspiration for the name is drawn from the technique of painters and construction workers who create extra flooring in the air in order to access a certain area in the work field. Vygotsky's ideas were considered controversial, particularly since he developed important psychological theory without any previous or formal psychological training.

Both the Zone of Proximal Development and the concept of Scaffolding introduced by Vygotsky represent examples of greater freedom the child can now access in his or her intellectual growth process.

Mooney (2000) closes this section of Vygotsky by telling us that for some teachers the idea that children can help each other learn is very freeing. They think back on the numerous times they've interrupted excellent opportunities for group learning by calling children to circle time where they are forced to sit and listen. Observing Vygotsky recommendations teachers have come to see that children learn not only by doing but also by talking, working with a peer and persisting until the task at hand is accomplished. It is this freedom to do and to learn through other means that Vygotsky strongly recommends (p. 92).

Erik Erikson is the last and youngest of these theorists introduced in this report and compared to Rousseau around the subject of more freedom and less power. Mooney (2000) tells us that he was born in Frankfurt Germany in 1902, that he was an artist and teacher who later became interested in psychology. Mooney also explains that Erikson's meeting and interacting with Anna Freud; the daughter of the great Sigmund Freud; played a role in persuading Erikson to study at the Vienna Psycho-analytic Institute where he specialized in child psycho-analysis (p.37). In a statement that may best define the notion of more freedom and less power Mooney (2000) presents Erikson telling us that parents, teachers and caretakers should learn to accept the child's swing between independence and dependence, and reassuring them that both are okay (47).

To the subject of freedom Erikson dedicates the third of his eight stages of development, pointing to the child of three to six years old, a period in which we encourage their fantasy, their curiosity and imagination. Like Rousseau, Erikson refers to this period as a time for play, not for formal education although in Rousseau's case this period is far more extensive.

The other group to which Erikson dedicates much of his attention on the subject to freedom, are the adolescents, particularly those within that group that may be confronting identity problems. It is at this stage between the ages of twelve and eighteen Erikson claims, that the child is confronted with a variety of social and moral issues. It is here that Erikson (1980) introduces us to the concept of a psychosocial moratorium. In this moratorium, the adolescent will use experimentation to grant themselves a prolongation of the interval between youth and adulthood with the purpose of finding a niche in which he or she may fit comfortably (175). Taking some time out, traveling to Europe, taking some time out to smell the roses or just taking some time out to get to know themselves and formulate their own ideas about the world, with ideas removed from that of their parents, peers or their particular culture group. In the final analysis this might be the strongest advocacy for freedom by any of the five theorists presented in this report.

There is a genuine sense of honesty that emanates from those committed to the development of children, and this palpable honesty has the ability to maintain the interest of scholars and researchers on the subject. It can be said, without any attempt at boldness, that the future of the specie is largely dependent on the proper development of those who constitute future leadership. The survival of the specie for the foreseeable future may not be in question, what may be questionable is the quality of life in this projected future, and this is very much dependent on the attention we pay to the development of children.

The five theorists presented here have done their part, and no doubt future theorists will continue to modify and improve on what those before them have worked so hard to put together.

VIOLENCE TOWARDS CHILDREN

After exploring some of the psychological reasons for parents' violence on children, this chapter will deal with the mechanism that allows some parents to reject the long-standing custom of disciplining their children by way of violence. Intended to be an active, functional document, the research will explore the persuasive language and instruments to be used in creating some ambivalence in those parents and other adults that steadfastly stand by the old customs of submitting children to adult's violence.

The epidemic of violence sweeping the world today has succeeded in tearing apart families and communities, stretching the resources of many social service agencies to its limits. This epidemic has also rendered vast sections of many countries around the world off limits and un-inhabitable to anyone with civilized behavior. Interestingly enough, this is not the first generation of humans grappling with wholesale gratuitous violence. Since the invention of weapons, humans have created extraordinary and sophisticated ways of hurting each other, a behavior that leads to many armed conflicts, and that is also intensified during the course of these conflicts. This wholesale violence took on new dimension with the invention of gunpowder, a product that became synonymous with facilitating killing. Repeated statements that weapons are not the cause of violence may have numbed our senses to these issues of violence and may have also reduced the responsibility we each have for studying this phenomenon, defining its cause and eventually bringing it under control.

The first question that is asked in this report is whether violence is just a by-product of the irresistible desire the strong has for taking advantage of the weak when the opportunity presents itself? Would this then be a confirmation of the violent nature of the species and that violence may be coded in our DNA?

The answers to these questions may never be found, but their absence behooves those of us who care about the future of the species to come together in the search for, or the formulation of.

Sigmund Freud, the celebrated father of psychology and psychoanalysis, dedicated little or none of his time or energy to the study of the cause of violence in humans, despite the fact that a massive war; and the horrible cruelty leading up to another; took place in his lifetime. Even with two world wars behind us, the species failed to produce an industry designed to steadily and consistently analyze the cause of violence in humans. Not until recently did it begin to dawn on a few psychologists that the cause of violence may be deeply rooted in childhood, that this strong desire to feel superior to other human beings may be really the cause of nearly all the misery we've heaped on each other since the dawn of civilization. The idea that these concepts are generated in us in our childhood years should be enough to give pause and take stock at the way we treat those human beings whose care we have been entrusted with.

This book is expected to be a significant part of the ongoing discussion on the subject of violence towards children as it implores the energy and engagement of everyone who shares the dream of a future world free of violence, convinced that the sacred concept of non-violence towards children begins in the home with the child. Non-violence in words, non-violence in deeds, and non-violence in actions.

The most unfortunate thing with the issue of the psychological reasons for violence towards children is that so few resources are available on the subject; it is almost as if writers and researchers have purposely stayed away from this extremely sensitive subject. Yet, it is the argument of so many that without willingness for open dialogue on the subject, the reality of our daily lives as it relates to violence, has reduced chances of ever improving.

Radda Barnen the Swedish version of *Save the Children* issued a pamphlet entitled *Hitting People Is Wrong - and Children Are People Too*. The pamphlet was later published by EPOCH (End Physical Punishment of Children) an informal alliance of organizations, which share the aim of ending all physical punishment of children by education and legal reform. The pamphlet is a list of six answers describing why parents hit children and in the final of these answers it states: "Many parents are under stress from difficult socio-economic conditions. Forbidding physical punishment would add to that stress and should await better standards of living." The pamphlet goes on to say—"This argument is a tacit admission of an obvious truth: physical punishment is often an outlet for the pent-up feelings of adults rather than an attempt to educate children" (p.1).

The article goes on to argue that in most parts of the world parents urgently need more social and economic support than they get, but they refuse to accept this behavior as justifications for venting their frustrations on children. They assert that children's protection from physical punishment must not be dependent on improvements in the socio-economic arrangements in their parents' lives. What is worse, they argue, hitting children is seldom an effective stress-reliever and cite as evident that most parents who hit out in temper experience guilt and wish that they could find other ways of disciplining their children.

The argument made by the pamphlet is that alternatives to physical punishments are not different punishments but an approach to 'discipline' which is positive rather than punitive, and they cite research showing that effective control of children's behavior does not depend upon punishment for wrong-doing but on clear and consistent limits that prevent it. They explain that adults modeling and an explanation of the behavior they would prefer for the child seems to have a more positive effect on curbing the child's behavior (p.2).

A more radical approach to this subject was offered by Jordan Riak head of the Parents and Teachers Against Violence. In the 1992 issue of the organization's newsletter, Riak published an essay entitled Plain Talk About Spanking and in the essay Riak argues that many spankers are habituated to the practice because it provides them with an instant outlet for their feelings of frustration and anger - not because they've found it an effective way to improve a child's behavior. The danger of this he argues, is that violence, by its very nature, tend to escalate as it is indulged in, thus making it impossible for there to be a safe way to hit a child (p.1).

Riak (1992), then goes on to make the connection between spanking and sexual molestation telling us that spanked children learn that their bodies are not their personal property, and that allowing someone else to do as they please with their bodies opens the gate for that someone or others to do the same or even more, and that even their sexual areas are subject to the will of adults. The child who submits to a spanking on Monday is not likely to say no to a molester on Tuesday. So, no matter what else violent parents think they are accomplishing with their behavior, they are setting children up to be easy prey for predators (p.2).

The other area in which those parents try to justify their behavior is arguing that the buttocks is safe because of its meaty structure but Riak then commented that medical science has long recognized and documented in great detail how being struck on the buttocks can stimulate sexual feelings. Riak (1992), makes it clear that located deep in the buttocks is the sciatic nerve, the largest nerve in the body and that a severe blow to the buttocks, particularly with a blunt instrument, could cause bleeding in the muscles that surround that nerve, possibly injuring it and causing impairment to the involved leg. Riak (1992), adds that a blow to the buttocks can cause injury to the tailbone (coccyx) or sacrum. It sends force waves upward through the spinal column possibly causing disc compression or compression fractures of vertebral bones. And as far as the old claim that God or nature intended that part of the anatomy for spanking Riak argues that that claim is brazenly perverse since no part of the human body was made to be mistreated (p.4).

The tragic consequence for many children who have been punished by spanking, according to Riak (1992), is that they form a connection between pain, humiliation and sexual arousal that endures for the rest of their lives. Riak then proceeds to introduce David Bakan, author of *Slaughter of the Innocents*, in which Bakan wrote:

> The buttocks are the locus for the induction of pain in a child. We are familiar with the argument that it is a safe

'locus' for spanking. However, the anal region is also the major erotic region at precisely the time the child is likely to be beaten there. Thus, it is aptly chosen to achieve the result of deranged sexuality in adulthood. (Bakan 1971 p. 113).

Riak (1992), continues to present the argument for no-spanking telling us that the pornography and prostitution industries do a thriving business catering to the needs of countless unfortunate individuals whose sexual development has been derailed by childhood spankings. If we put all other considerations aside, this should be reason enough never to spank a child (p.5).

The excuse that so many schools give that the hands are safe for hitting is also refuted by Riak (1992), stating that his research has revealed that the child's hand is particularly vulnerable because its ligaments, nerves, tendons and blood vessels are close to the skin, which has no underlying protective tissue. Striking the hands of younger children is especially dangerous to the growth plates in the bones, which, if damaged, can cause deformity or impaired function. Striking a child's hand can also cause fractures, dislocations and can lead to premature osteoarthritis, he argues. Many of us have also become familiar with the shaking baby syndrome, but not everyone has. Shaking a baby that is crying annoyingly seems innocuous to many uninformed parents specially those parents in the lower strata of our society, and those in the developing world, so the damage or death to those children will forever go undetected (p.5).

Riak (1992), ends his comments by telling us that we should not be surprised that many youngsters reject the adult world to the degree they believe it has rejected them. Nor should we be surprised that those who throughout childhood have been recipients of violence will become dispensers of it as soon as they are able. Some teachers work tirelessly to curb violence-impacted children's aggressiveness, to instill trust which those children lack, and to redirect their energies in positive directions but that is a daunting task even for the most dedicated and best prepared teachers since it requires extraordinary resources currently inaccessible to the current public-school systems. School dropout, addiction and delinquency would cease to be major problems if only it were possible to persuade parents and other caretakers to stop socializing children in ways likely to make them antisocial and/or self-destructive (p. 6).

FEMALE GENITAL MUTILATION

With the exception of outright murder, which was committed systematically against children just a few short centuries ago, Female Genital Mutilation is regarded by its victims as the worst form of violence.

It could be said that outside of crimes like rape, incest and brutal beatings in which the child survives physically, hardly anything compares with this supposedly well meaning but grossly misguided adults who butcher the private parts of an innocent little girl in the name of culture. In fact that is the excuse commonly offered for the lack of intervention in this practice, making an assault on a person acceptable only by invoking the word culture. Described by the literature and by the victims, only rape and murder can surpass the horrors of Female Genital Mutilation. Frye (2004) commented although Female Genital Mutilation is sometimes referred to as female circumcision, perhaps as a way of sanitizing the concept and to make it more acceptable in the minds of the readers for the horrors it entails would be an assault on the senses. She chose to use the full expression Female Genital Mutilation because it demands of the reader and the researchers a complete understanding of the horrors some preteen girl is undergoing even at the moment they are consuming the information. Female Genital Mutilation is primarily practiced in parts of Africa, the Middle East, Asia and some islands in the Pacific some of it is now being seen in the United States, the United Kingdom and other Western countries as immigrants bring with them their degrading practices. She offers the World Health Organization's 2008 report that approximately 140 million women and girls worldwide have undergone Female Genital Mutilation since they began keeping track, and that even though its prevalence in the United Stated is unknown, given the 2004 reports from the Center for Reproductive Rights, women in Western countries are currently at great risk of being subjected to these practices. What is interesting is that the World Health Organization has concluded in its 2008 report that there are no health benefits to this practice and that it constitutes in every sense a violation of human rights. While some say that Female Genital Mutilation should be prohibited globally because of its barbarity and because it constitutes one of the worse forms of child abuse, there are those who argue that it is a rite of passage that needs to be observed in order to preserve cultural identity. (Frye 2004, Barstow 1999).

Frye (2004) presents the history of Female Genital Mutilation as a practice that dates back more than 5,000years, one that may have had its origins in ancient Egypt. Details of how it came about were not offered but he stated that from the examinations of ancient Egyptian mummies, there is evidence that Female Genital Mutilation was practiced routinely.

Religious people supporting FGM claim that their religious texts require these physical alterations as they are a necessity in securing a woman her standing within her community. FGM goes beyond circumcision in removing the male aspect from a woman and further instills her femininity as she defines herself as a woman that is now more enhanced, docile and obedient as a result. Currently, African culture works to uphold a male-dominated society. This precedent is not in line with the goals of the lAC as its goals work to establish a more equal role for both males and females. Not wanting to alienate itself from the general public, the lAC uses mildly aggressive tactics to induce cooperation and advance the woman's role in African culture (Frye 2004).

Despite the perception of Female Genital Mutilation as a foreign practice, its other name, Clitoridectomies; was practiced routinely in the United States and Europe to treat lesbianism, hysteria, melancholy, epilepsy and excessive masturbation as recently as the late nineteenth century, in fact she added, the practice continued in the U.S. until the late 1930s when an outrage public demanded its abolishment. The author added that despite the belief by many that Female Genital Mutilation is a religiously related practice, in actuality the practice is not associated with any specific religious faith and there are no religious scripts that proscribe this barbarous act. It has been illegal in Britain since 1985, she tells us but it is still practiced secretly in some immigrant communities, and when that proves too risky, girls are sent abroad to have the procedure thereby skirting the legal restrictions. In 1997 and again in 2008, the World Health Organization issued a joint statement with the United Nations to support increased advocacy for the abandonment of the practice of Female Genital Mutilation enlightening the public as to the intricacies of the practice. They describe it as characterize by four distinct types: The first is a Clitoridectomy, a procedure that partially or totally removes the clitoris. The second type, Excision, is the partial or total removal of the clitoris and labia minor which may include incision of the labia major. The third is, Infibulations, the narrowing of the vaginal opening through the creation of a "covering seal," which is formed by cutting and repositioning the inner, and sometimes outer labia. Sometimes this includes removal of the clitoris and sometimes it does not. A fourth category is preserved for other, which includes any harmful, non-medical procedure done involuntarily to the female genitalia such. (Frye 2004).reports that in the past Female Genital Mutilation has been carried out by a female circumciser, that the procedure was done without anesthetic, antiseptics, or antibiotics often in unsanitary conditions utilizing instruments such knifes, razors, pieces of glass or sharpened stones, instruments that were likely to be dirty, having been used on other girls and never sanitized. She goes on to report that even though the procedure is being done by trained medical personnel in a few places around the world, it continues to be an act that results in permanent physical mutilation to the child, one that changes body functions forever, with immediate complications and extreme pain in all cases, not to mention shock, hemorrhaging, tetanus, sepsis, urine retention, open sores and injury to nearby genital tissue. Other long-term consequences include recurrent bladder and urinary tract infections, cysts, infertility, need for later surgeries, increased risk of childbirth complications and newborn deaths. In nearly all cases, a host of surgeries may be required in later years to allow for sexual intercourse or for a pregnant woman to deliver a child. On a nonphysical level the psychological consequences of this traumatic experience is one that is yet to be fully analyzed, but reports of post-traumatic stress disorder, anxiety, depression and psychosexual problems are fairly common. (Frye 2004) ponders the psychological dilemma that allows these victims to subject other little girls to the same procedure just a few short years after their own trauma. Arguments such as female rite of passage, custom and tradition, the clitoris is dirty or evil, the clitoris will grow too long, non-excised women will be barren, the clitoris causes male impotence, it insures virginity and chastity, women who have not undergone the procedure are rejected as marriage partners, it increases a woman's femininity, it prevents social ostracism, it controls the female sex drive, it prevents lesbianism, it ensures paternity, it calms the female personality, it defines cultural identity, it encourages cultural cohesion; have long been offered to justify the procedure. Those who argue for the abolition of this barbarous procedure are accused by its defenders of ethnocentrism, cultural imperialism and cultural imposition, as they assert their rights to continue subjecting defenseless little girls to this ancient procedure. Frye (2004) alludes to the procedure as a gender-specific human rights violation and a form of child abuse reflecting a deep-rooted inequality between the sexes, and an extreme form of discrimination against women, adding that the fact that the practice is specific to certain cultural groups should not excuse it from international scrutiny. Healthcare professionals worldwide are charged with the responsibility of taking a stand on this issue, and to understand the abhorrence of this practice. The author concludes that culture should be progressive beneficial and not static or retrogressive to the detriment of those who by mere accident of birth belong to a practicing clan, that certain cultural rituals found at odds with the fundamental rights of individuals are being discarded as the global village shrinks in the face of rapid technological advancement. She argues that Female Genital Mutilation should incur global abolition the same way other anachronistic global tradu cultural practices have, *ie*; that it must be abolished because it is a violation of human rights. In an apparent invocation of cowardice Barstow (1999) charged that the human species has habitually exhibited cruelty towards its weaker members, notably women, children and the elderly (p. 73) and goes on to say that development in human rights around the globe has brought much attention to the wanton violence, sexual violence, deprivation, oppression and outright murder committed against women everywhere (p.155). With the adopting of the Convention on the Rights of the Child in 1959 the general assembly of the United Nations has cast its lot on the side of children irrespective of cultural norms or beliefs. The measure states explicitly that all nations must take measures to abolish traditional practices that are damaging to the health of children.   In a letter to the editor in the March April (1997) issue of the Canadian Journal of Public Health, men pay high dowry for women who have undergone Female Genital Mutilation as they've acquired a woman who had not been penetrated by other men before him, but it is obvious they're not   aware of the health consequences, and why their partners suffer from multiple health problems.

The perpetuation of this practice is a stark reminder of our savage nature as a species. All of our bragging and self-adulations are just hallow mockery in light of the things we tolerate particularly against the weak and the defenseless.

We are each equally guilty for tolerating it.

RADICAL NON-VIOLENCE
THE NEW PARADIGM

In our times the term radical has taken on new and more perverse meaning for even though its *Latin* etymology is Radix or
root, today the term has come to describe the most dogmatic, violent and narrow-minded elements within a particular religion.
Despite that unfortunate reality, we are not yet willing to give up
on the term, because it allows us to understand the origins and
root causes of any issue.

Radical non-violence begins with an extraordinary respect for
all living things, especially the small and defenseless. We carefully avoid the term love because that too has been misunderstood and misused. You simply cannot love someone and mis-
treat them at the same time, another word must be invented if we
are to mix mistreatment with love. Respect however, carries no
emotions, focusing solely on the intrinsic value of the person or
living being regardless of its size. It is virtually impossible to
hurt; physically or otherwise; that which we happen to respect.

Real non-violence represents a paradigm shift in the ways that
human beings relate to each other. In this case it may also be referred to as radical non-violence because of its focus on the root
causes of the anger and vitriol that seems to characterize human
interactions.

Humanity has had three renowned non-violent advocates: the
Palestinian Jesus Christ, the Hindu Mahatma Gandhi and African
American Martin Luther King, and it is likely that there be a great
many others dedicated to the cause of non-violence who we
simply did not become aware of. Violence towards children was

as prevalent in their times as it was in any other, yet in none of these cases have we read of a denunciation of that violence that is perpetrated against children or a recognition of the damaging effects of this violence. In his 1974 publication *The History of Childhood* Lloyd deMause reminds us that at the time of Jesus' birth, infanticide was a common practice throughout the world, including the Middle East, and that his brief presence on this planet had no effect whatsoever on this horrifying practice. DeMause (1974) reminds us that sealing children in the walls and foundations of bridges and buildings to strengthen the structure was also common. From the building of the wall of Jericho to as late as 1843 in Germany (p.27). Likewise, we find none of Gandhi's writings reflects a specific interest in the safety and protection of children, the same is true for the writings issued by and about Martin Luther King.

This new approach to non-violence is unprecedented, it gives personhood to the child and it calls on civilized people to address the child's behavior clinically utilizing the techniques developed after more than two centuries of psychological practices.

It is the responsibility of every legitimate government to guarantee the safety and security of all of its citizens, particularly the most vulnerable. Fortunately, state and local governments around the world have been responding to the United Nations 1978 Declaration of the Right of the Child which says in essence that all children deserve to live in safety and security.

The goal is non-violence in the home, particularly with respect to children, and we believe that governments have it within their powers to provide incentives for parents who sign on to this

agreement. Tax breaks, food surplus programs, high school di-
plomas or college credits for those who successfully comply are
but a few of the options that with some creativity, government
can make available to these parents and caretakers who have
done their part in helping to create better citizens. However, this
will not happen by itself, with this priority in mind, future organ-
izers will learn to bring pressure to bear on both elected and appointed officials at all level of government to endorse these creative ideas whose ultimate effect will drastically reduce social
problems and create a more functional citizenry.

Partnering with parents is essential to providing greater security for children, but for those parents who are already borderline
dysfunctional or those whose method of discipline is deeply engrained, it will require a great deal of persuasion to convince
them of the benefits of a new approach to raising their children.
Children who have been raised successfully without corporal
punishment may be the ambassadors for engaging other parents
in an effort to persuade them as to the benefits of this non-violent
approach to child rearing, for if parents become convinced that
their children can do as well without the use of violence there is
a chance they will consider this method particularly when the by-
product of this new method is in their presence. Many of the parents who need to be dissuaded from the old methods are themselves functionally illiterate, so volumes of written materials may
not be useful in this case, it will require a core of committed or-
ganizers that includes adolescents, concerned mothers, seniors
and anyone else with the ability to persuade, to reach out to these
parents and caretakers and convince them as to the validity of this
new method.

The concluding thought in this chapter is that only a, well-structured campaign against violence can really begin to force parents and other caregivers to take a second look at their behavior, and in the process, to contemplate other avenues for raising their children. It is expected that at some point the United States will join the other twenty-nine nations that have passed laws against corporal punishment, and when it does, this will become an added component to the persuasive mechanisms currently in place to guard the safety of children and the healthy survival of our society. For now, we can view this as the most compelling and most satisfying of all endeavors.

RELIGIOUS INDOCTRINATION
AND ITS IMPACT ON THE CHILD

Before embarking on the subject that encompasses the form of indoctrination most of us are familiar with; that is religious indoctrination; it is important to attempt a definition of the term itself and the various ways in which it has been utilized in the past. There is no question that over the years we have had a variety of definitions for the term. Barrow et, al (2010) comments that much of it depends on the academic level of the person offering the definition, or their political or intellectual inclinations. In offering a generalized and perhaps more generic definition for the term, we can safely say that it is a process in which coercion, persuasion and often compulsion, are used to introduce an idea or belief system to an individual or group of individuals. In this definition, a key component to the process invariably, is the absence of critical examination or questioning on the part of the new adherents. Barrow et al (2010), comments that the term has obtained a strong pejorative tinge in the educational discourse particularly because of the absence of critical thinking and questioning the term is associated with. Barrow et al (2010) tell us that the term is often contrasted with the grand ideas of autonomy and open-mindedness that our society has come to expect from any form of positive instruction (p. 279).

Religious indoctrination on the other hand, involves a particular effort to have its adherents submit to a prescribe set of narrow and irrational beliefs that invariably involves a concept of god as an image or person to be adored, to be in awe of, or to be

64

fearful of. The proven and tested method is to implant these dogmas in the minds of the individual long before he or she achieves the capacity to discern the process for themselves, thus preempting all possibilities for resistance.

In their own analysis of this subject, Barrow and Woods (2006) introduce us to the term "unshakable belief", related to the intentions of the indoctrinator's intent. Getting someone to believe in a proposition that is lacking in proof or evidence is at the heart of the process of indoctrination. Barrow and Woods (2006) remind us that the essence of indoctrination is not to be found in the degree of conviction but in the blind unshakable commitment. It possesses something that is beyond argument, and beyond reasoning, that is its position as being antithetical to education (p. 71). Barrow and Woods (2006) tell us that there are things in the world that are different from education and even incompatible with it in certain areas, but indoctrination is education inverted. It involves denial of the value of rationality, a real phenomenon that we must contend with for reasons that are too numerous to list (p. 71). To be honorably committed to a cause is one thing, but indoctrination is clearly another level of functioning, one that requires much more of our attention. The term unshakable belief reminds us of the extraordinary efforts the neurological system had to make to accept irrational thoughts.

In contemplating the Christian symbol of a gentle Jesus, meek and mild one has to wonder if the violent scenarios described in Reuters (2004) could be tolerated within Christianity. The stories of violence described in the first half of the Christian bible known

as the Old Testament are a possible example of the similarity between the Abrahamic faiths and why this phenomenon may not
be inconceivable and violence

One is compelled to wonder about the effects strong and violent biblical statements have on the minds of children that are
under the indoctrination of religion, particularly the Abrahamic
faiths.

Children brought up in the Christian tradition and instructed
to read the bible are compelled to make sense of this aspect of
their religion. The notion of an all-loving god comes into question for them and in many cases the entire foundation of their
belief system crumbles.

The writings in these chapters and verses vary according to the
version of the bible the person may be in possession of, thus, one
is free to consult the versions of their choice or a few versions,
for that matter, for the purpose of comparison. These writings
contained in the bible have been condemned by some for their
irrationality and dismissed by others as insignificant but rarely
are they analyzed for the effects they have on the minds of the
masses, particularly on the children's.

The task of exploring the role of religion in human progress
or non-progress is a rather difficult one, one that requires an overwhelming degree of what is referred to as intellectual honesty,
that is, a willingness to explore areas that are considered off limits to most humans, and confront what are considered established
norms. Because of that, realistic research on a subject such as
religion is all the more challenging and for it we must thank the
few daring researchers, who risk so much to stare down and confront established norms. Old friends for daring to challenge the

sacred have cast many off as pariahs and others were shunned by colleagues and other professionals, as they embarked on a subject matter that made them uneasy. To add to that, the few who would in the past dare to venture into these delicate areas would often do so denouncing the established order as well as its administrators, by-passing the critical mass of thinkers required to have some impact on the subject. This denunciation and open confrontation has led to confusion rather than clarity, particularly for those tapped under the influence of a rather powerful socio-political infrastructure. The result of this of course, is limited research material on a subject of this nature. There are researchers and academicians dedicated to this subject but their numbers are limited, and since the first label attached to anyone who dares to take on this subject is that of atheist, there is a considerable reduction in the pool of intellectuals willing to go that far.

No other generation in the past has had this much exposure to scientific facts and evidence surrounding the presence of humans in this universe. If for no other reason than that, we owe it to ourselves to persuade families of all religious inclination or none at all, to guarantee that these facts are not hidden from their children.

SCIENTIFIC PSYCHOLOGY

Scientific Psychology sets as a premise for its intervention with human beings a working knowledge of the intricacies surrounding the origins of planet Earth, and the significance of this knowledge to the psychodynamics of the individual.

For nearly a century, scientists have argued that approximately 13 billion years ago an explosion took place that would culminate in the formation of stars and planets in infinite numbers. The first to formulate a theory with some resemblance to that was the English philosopher, theologian, and scientist Robert Grosseteste (1175-1253) who in his 1225 treatise *on the subject of light* explored the nature of matter and the cosmos. He described the birth of the universe in an explosion and the crystallization of matter to form stars and planets. He was referred to by many as the real founder of the tradition of scientific thought in medieval Oxford, and in some ways, of the modern English intellectual tradition.

Nearly 700 years later Monsignor Georges Lemaitre (1894-1966) a Belgian Catholic priest, astronomer and professor of physics at the Catholic University of Leuven arrived at a similar conclusion. He was the first to derive what is now known as Hubble's law and made the first estimation of what is now called the Hubble constant, which he published in 1927. Lemaitre is credited for having coined the phrase *Primeval Atom* and the *Cosmic Egg* to conceptualize the theory of the birth of the Universe.

The story here is that 2 highly positioned religious scientists, one English and the other Belgian were the authors of the big bang theory even though they were 700 years apart. This alone should end the non-existing rivalry between religion and science that we are eternally beset with.

Notwithstanding the fact that these theories were first presented by religious men for largely religious audiences, the theory itself is still difficult for most human minds to fathom. Endless questions about the source of that *Primordial Atom or that cosmic egg* that brought on the explosion would abound.

Accepting the notion of unfathomability that the scientist theory of the Big Bang brought us, contained within that story is one that is immensely more palatable to the average human mind. Those same scientists tell us that 8 billion years after that explosion (5 billion years ago), a cloud of cosmic dust and gases called a Nebula was formed on the outskirts of one of the billions of galaxies that makes up the Universe. One of those billions of galaxies is the one we belong to call the Milky Way. The nebula formed within its limits was replete with Hydrogen, Oxygen, Helium, Nitrogen and other elements. Gravity slowly drew the gas molecules together to form a spinning disk that sucked in even more hydrogen creating a great deal of pressure and heat at its center. These hydrogen molecules eventually fused to each other, igniting later and giving birth to a new star that is our sun. The debris present at the birth of our sun coalesced to form what we now know as planets, and the mass of the sun created a field of gravity that kept them swirling around it. One of those of course was to become our own planet Earth.

The planet remained a ball of fire for its first 2.5 billion years achieving temperatures that could sustain life only 2 billion years ago. Continuous bombardment of icy comets not only assisted in the cooling of the planet but assisted in the formation of its oceans.

In revealing to us that these chemical compounds: Carbon, Hydrogen, Oxygen, Nitrogen, Helium, and a few others are the building blocks of life and that they are found everywhere in the Universe, these scientists have really solved the major question facing all of humanity, *i.e.* What is life and how was it generated. With the information they provided we can deduce that life is an extraordinary combination of some of the most vital compounds found in the Universe. The fact that said experiment first took place in the waters of the newly formed oceans should not surprise us since water itself make up two of those chemical elements, Hydrogen and Oxygen. The combination of 2 molecules of Hydrogen and 1 molecule of Oxygen produces exactly that, water. There the first unicellular forms appeared more than four hundred million years ago, eventually growing lungs and legs to eventually step out of those waters to explore earth's vegetation. These first reptilian forms took on various sizes according to the conditions on the land.

The information these scientists revealed has also helped to confront our most dreadful fear, *death*. It begins with their definition of life as energy, adding further that in this Universe of ours, energy never dies that it simply transforms, mutating from one form into another. In other words, at the time our hearts stop permanently and we cease to breathe indefinitely, that energy is somewhere else participating in other functions.

On the question of life elsewhere in the Universe these scientists remind us that we are essentially star dust, that the same chemical materials found in our star is found in us, and that if that is so for our solar system why wouldn't it be for the other infinite number of solar systems that make up the Universe. The key element here is distance.

Our own star is 93 million miles away, but the second closest is Alfa Centaury at a distance of 4.37 light years away. To begin an understanding of this distance one must first understand that a light year is the distance light travels in the span of a year and the simple measurement of that distance begins with the understanding of the distance light travels in one second. The rest is simple multiplication as we do 186.000 x 60 x 60 x 24 x 365. Take that number and multiply it times 4.37 years and we get the distance that is to be covered to approach our nearest star. Traveling at the speed of light in little under 4 and a half years we'll make it to the vicinity of Alfa Centauri.

PSYCHOTHERAPY
AND THE HEALING PROCESS

This book attempts to present a comprehensive review of the process we have come to know as psychotherapy, its history and the contribution it has made to overall human happiness and the advancement of the species. Dr. Jerome Frank's 1963 publication *Persuasion and Healing,* in which he compares the various therapeutic approaches of the past fifty years, will serve as a point of departure as I explore the multicultural dimension of the psychotherapeutic process, and the effectiveness of its application in a cross-cultural setting.

Reasoning and introspection therefore, it can be argued, are the foundations for philosophy, as humans began to ask questions regarding themselves and their environment, their origin, and their destiny. This deep thinking also gave way to the discipline we have come to know as psychology, a Greek term for the study of the soul. (*Psyche = the Soul Logos = Study*).

A clear understanding of what we have come to know as the helping profession is important if we are to make these services available to a larger number of people in our society, recognize the generalized emotional malady that touches nearly everyone and eventually improve the efficacy of the healing that so many are so desperately in search of.

The blurring of the line that separates facts from fiction creates a never ending and violent conflict inside the mind of many individuals, and this conflict leads to the type of confusion that effectively serves the interest of those with answers for which there are no evidences. These individuals, or groups as the case may be, use this confusion to their advantage promoting their brand of truth thus increasing the sense of guilt and confusion among the confused and most self-harming behaviors are the result of confusion.

Psychologists and philosophers are yet to define ignorance and manipulation as the nemesis threatening sanity, security, world peace and individual happiness. Until they do, the revolving doors of therapeutic and behavioral centers everywhere may be swinging perpetually.

Distinguishing the two and acting both forcefully and legally in the construct of that distinction is the psychologists' greatest challenge.

But for a thorough understanding of the practice we have come to know as psychotherapy it is important to take a closer look at what we have come to know so far as human history, bearing in mind all of its contradictions and polemics surrounding the topic.

Homo sapiens is the term used to describe the creatures invested with the ability to reason, with the capacity for introspection and with the ability to resolve problems. To that, we may add language, although a voice box and vocal chords came sometime after Homo sapiens developed basic problem-solving skills.

With the rapid changes in technology and a transient society moving at speeds that very few are able to keep up with, there may never have been as great a demand for the therapeutic process and the sense of wellness it is expected to provide. Everyone from the high-powered executive to the housewife, the lawyer, the builder, the doctor, and professions of all sorts, are all in need of the assertiveness and the coping mechanisms provided by those who are engaged in the helping profession.

Psychology is still in the process of defining itself and fending off critics who still attempt to write the profession off as quackery or pseudoscience. However, for those who have assisted another human being in becoming even slightly more functional in a world overrun by madness, uncertainty and confusion, their feelings about this profession is an entirely different one.

These brave soldiers in the battle for clarity, understanding and self-realization for others, are the ultimate helpers, in need of no gratitude or rewards as they commit to their best efforts in improving the lives of those who seek them out for assistance.

ADDICTION TREATMENT
AND THE POLITICS OF DRUGS

A Non-Governmental Organization committed to empowering its members intellectually would not be complete without an analysis of the impact of illicit drugs, not just in our society but in world we inhabit. Illicit drugs impact those we serve so it is inevitable that we take the time out to do a careful analysis of this subject, and define the attitude our organization intends to maintain on the subject. It goes without saying that the widespread violence produced by the illicit drug trade is not limited to the United States, here children caught in the cross fires of gang wars are being killed nearly every day, but the scenario appears to be even worse in countries south of the United States and the Caribbean where young people compete for the opportunity to get their products to the drug abusing market that exists in the United States. A necessary component of intellectual pursuit is recognizing the reality of the social environment, for despite our efforts to promote intellectual growth and intellectual empowerment, recognizing the allure of the lucrative business of drug trafficking represents, in many cases a nearly insurmountable hurdle in our efforts to reach a good many adolescents. This reality compels us to revisit and discuss ideas like de-penalization, de-criminalization and even legalization as it relates to drugs, ideas that can only be discussed adequately by individuals with advanced intellect.

An additional damage caused by our policy towards drugs is that human beings seeking to escape the crime ridden areas of countries south of the United States, will head for the only country they can gain access to for their mere economic survival, but when they pursue that only option they are immediately made criminals by virtue of their survival effort. When they're caught and eventually sent back to their country of origin, made uninhabitable by the trafficking and violence they originally attempted to escape, desolation, desperation and crime often becomes their only survival option.

As we contemplate the three words mentioned earlier: de-penalization, de-criminalization and legalization, it may help to take a look at the societies that have experimented with these concepts. We've all become familiar with the case of the Netherlands where are reported to be using at will, the kinds of drugs that are illegal in the United States. The opinions vary widely as to the actual results of the Netherlands experiment in drug accessibility, but a more recent experiment with drug accessibility was put into practice in Portugal, highly controversial in nature and with a great deal of predictions regarding its impending failure. Yet in an article published in the April 7, 2009 issue of *Scientific America* entitled, Five Years After: Portugal's Drug Decriminalization Policy Shows Positive Results, writer Brian Vastag argues that since the beginning of the experiment in 2001street drug related death from drug overdose fell significantly, as did the cases of new HIV infection for in the face of a growing number of deaths and cases of HIV linked to drug abuse, the Portuguese government in 2001 tried a new tack to get a handle on the problem—it decriminalized the use and possession of heroin, cocaine, marijuana, LSD and other illicit street drugs. Five years later, the number of deaths from street drug overdose dropped from around 400 to 290 annually, and the number of new HIV cases caused by using dirty needles to inject heroin, cocaine and other illegal substances plummeted from nearly 1,400 in 2000 to about 400 in 2006. The focus was on treatment and prevention instead of jailing users would decrease the number of deaths and infections, so instead of being put into prison, addicts are going to treatment centers and they're learning how to control their drug usage or getting off drugs entirely. Vastag (2009) then goes on to give some details of the Portuguese experiment, telling us that under the 2001 law, penalties for people caught dealing and trafficking drugs are unchanged; that dealers are still jailed and subjected to fines depending on the crime. But people caught using or possessing small amounts—defined as the amount needed for 10 days of personal use—are brought before what's known as a "Dissuasion Commission," a special administrative body made up of three persons. That there were several of these commissions each including at least one lawyer or judge and one health care or social worker. As it stands, Vastag (2009) tells us, the panel has the option of recommending treatment, a small fine, or no sanctions whatsoever. Vastag (2009) then citesWalter Kemp, a spokesperson for the United Nations Office on Drugs and Crime, stating that decriminalization in Portugal "appears to be working and that his office is putting more emphasis on improving health outcomes, such as reducing needle-borne infections. Drug legalization, argues Vastag (2009), removes all criminal penalties for producing, selling and using drugs; no country has tried it. In contrast, decriminalization, as practiced in Portugal, eliminates jail time for drug users but maintains criminal penalties for dealers. Spain and Italy have also decriminalized personal use of drugs and Mexico's president has proposed doing the same (p. 1). The August 29, 2009 issue of *Economist*, published an article entitled: Treating, not punishing. A specific author was not mentioned for the article but it made continuous reference to a study done by *constitutional lawyer* Glenn Greenwald regarding the Portuguese experiment with drug decriminalization. In it Greenwald is said to be arguing that the evidence from Portugal since 2001 is that decriminalization of drug use and possession has many benefits and no harmful side-effects, despite the fact that in 2001 newspapers around the world carried graphic reports of addicts injecting heroin in the grimy streets of a Lisbon slum. When a young British backpacker was found comatose on a Lisbon street corner, the government took action, and the result was a sweeping decriminalization law. The personal use and possession of all drugs, including heroin and cocaine was allowed. The foreign media expressed concerns that holiday resorts would become dumping-grounds for drug tourists. Some conservative politicians went as far as denouncing it as lunacy, convinced that plane loads of foreign students would head for the Algarve to smoke marijuana. The report then assesses Portuguese drug policy in the context of the EU's approach to drugs. The varying legal frameworks, as well as the overall trend toward liberalization, are examined to enable a meaningful comparative assessment between Portuguese data and data from other EU states. Greenwald's conclusion was that judged by virtually every metric, the Portuguese decriminalization framework has been a resounding success, and that within this success lie self-evident lessons that should guide drug policy debates around the world (p. 1).

Even the United Nation has weighed in on the Portuguese experiment. In an article appearing in the June 24, 2009 edition of the *Huntington Post,* writer Ryan Grim commented that, in an about face, the United Nations praised drug decriminalization in its annual report on the state of global drug policy. This is significant because in previous years the UN drug *czar* had expressed skepticism about Portugal's decriminalization, which had removed criminal penalties in 2001 for personal drug possession and emphasized treatment over incarceration, and that the policy was in violation of international drug treaties, but after a mission to Portugal in 2004 the International Narcotics Control Board noted that the acquisition, possession and abuse of drugs had remained prohibited, and commented that the practice of exempting small quantities of drugs from criminal prosecution is consistent with the international drug control treaties. Grim (2009) commented that the Executive Director of the United Nations Office of Drugs and Crime Antonio Maria Costa has been exploring the debate over repealing drug controls, acknowledging that attempts to control the flow and use of drugs have generated an illicit black market of macro-economic proportions that uses violence and corruption as its primary tools. Grim (2009) added that despite Costa's openness on the subject, Jack Cole, executive director of Law Enforcement Against Prohibition (LEAP) and a retired undercover narcotics detective, objected to the report's classification of current policy as *control* commenting that the world's 'drug czar,' Costa would have you believe that the legalization movement is calling for the abolition of drug control, but the opposite is true he added, we are demanding that governments replace the failed policy of prohibition with a system that actually regulates and controls drugs, including their purity and prices,   as well as who produces them and who they can be sold to. You can't have effective control under prohibition, as we should have learned from our failed experiment with alcohol in the U.S. between 1920 and 1933.

EDUCATION

There is a revolution under way today as it relates to the subject of education. This revolution is propelled by technology, and the extraordinary tool given to us by scientists around the world who came together to create what we know today as the *World Wide Web.*

No doubt this magnificent technology is being abuse today by many, some to express their ignorance and their antipathy for science, even as they exploit its benefits. But thanks to the *World Wide Web,* the International Center for Intellectual Development is bringing all levels of valuable education to the homes of children and adults around the world.

Our motto is a simple one: The lack of money shall no longer be an excuse for those who wish to advance academically.

Our contention is that everything a child needs to learn before entering higher learning; post-secondary education that is; can be learned in less than 13 years.

The rationale behind this statement is a simple one, the growing numbers of gifted children in the public and private school system have demonstrated that this is indeed an achievable goal.

The argument is that stimulated minds can assimilate far more information that we thought previously, and in this era of advanced information at everyone's fingertip, languishing in and outdated school system with some of the most backward administrators and teachers is nothing short of punishment to a child.

Irreparable damage is done to a child's developing mind when he or she is taught mythology as real history. If Abraham, Moses and Jesus are mythical characters, introducing them to young minds as historic figures is grossly unfair to that child's mental development. That if the child's mind is entangled with a story that is a complete fabrication, we cannot expect it to grow. That mind cannot be expected to adhere to advanced reasoning and analysis if it is unable to distinguish facts from fiction. That mind is therefore easily manipulated by others who are not subjected to childlike thoughts and beliefs.

The world is on fire with deep unrest in nearly every country, and once again young people are being murdered by their own governments simply because of speaking out. Among them there are a few who have overcome the ***Religious Tyranny*** that nearly all young minds are subjected to, but the vast majority are still proud believers. They simply cannot see the relationship between their adherence to nonsense and their state of oppression. They're unable to understand that for the most part they are their own worst enemies.

Given the plethora of gods, 2.500 and counting, and the plethora of religions 4.500 and counting, one can understand the stranglehold these belief systems have on the minds of those masses that also yearn for liberation and a better life. They cannot achieve those goals because they are in fact program through these belief systems to work against themselves.

The real revolution begins when the species abolishes religion, until then it is just empty noise with plenty of young people getting killed. With their blessings, their governments have given over the world's wealth to a few individuals, the so-called one percent, and that is never going to change. Not unless one of these generations remove the blinders and take complete and permanent control of the political systems currently controlled by the Kleptocrats in control of our lives.

Making a few substances illegal for human use on increases its value, and this sets us up for the game that is currently plaid between the powerful merchants of death, and the politicians they control. That industry is present in nearly every country, and with the Kleptocrats pretending to control it the problem can only get worse.

At the time of this writing a psychological crisis is brewing among young African American males convinced that their lives can be snuffed out at whim by any European American law officer, but also by any European American with a gun. The only justification that needs to be presented for this is that they were in fear of their lives.

The religious and the academic institutions are at a loss for answers as it relates to this crisis. As an organization, our only answer to this crisis for the time being is a renewed focus on education, not just conventional education with its road blocks and unnecessary delays, but a revolutionary approach to education that guarantees a motivated student a clear path to a PhD. There have not been any reported cases of a doctor of philosophy gunned down for any reason whatsoever regardless of the circumstances. For one, not only do they not put themselves in situations where they can be easily gunned down, but as professionals, they are better prepared to de-escalate any human situation, and fully prepared to handle crisis without emotions. No doubt this is a long-term plan, unlikely to save the life of the young man who is scheduled to be gunned down by a zealous cop tomorrow or a poisoned racist who will seize on the opportunity the current racist climate offers him or her to take a Black life with impunity.

Given the mission of this organization the curriculum for these degrees leans heavily towards science and psychology, and that is because these two areas of study allow its professionals to bring clarity and direction to those in its search. By their very nature, and for the mission that is embarked on, these two areas of study that are wide in their scope, offer job security for nearly everyone involved. The hate, confusion, misinformation, depression and low self-esteem among the masses in our times almost guarantees this.

THE ORIGINS OF MONEY AND WEALTH

From his home in Osaka Japan the researcher James Corbett has engaged in the analysis of a host of contemporary subjects of sociopolitical and economic nature, two of which we present in this publication. In analyzing the origins of the Federal Reserve Board Corbett wrote in 2014 that the economic/financial institution that controls money in the United States, and money in the world for that matter, had a rather surreptitious and insidious beginning. The piece is called: Century of Enslavement and it begins it with an extract from a letter in which president Roosevelt complains to Colonel House that the financial institutions are running the government.

In asking the question: What is money and where does it come from? Corbett receives a series of answers none of which gets to the root of the matter. He goes to the heart of the question of why the subject of the origins of money is so fastidiously avoided by old and young alike regardless of their levels of education. He adds that our monetary ignorance is really by design, that it is really a smokescreen created for the purpose of keeping the average person confused on that subject because everyone is clear on the fact that the subject is important. So if it is this confusing it has to be because someone wants it to be so. At the moment it presents itself as a giant jigsaw puzzle, but the pieces of this giant jigsaw puzzle begin to fall in place when we take a close look at the Federal Reserve Bank, how it was created and who had the most interest in its creation.

Reason dictates that for any country to operate effectively there must be a fiduciary institution that regulates the complex system of exchange of goods and services, and that this agency must be public in nature, heavily controlled by both the public and the government. That agency is expected to manage money and monetary policy, preserve the purchasing power of the currency of the nation, and ensure that a sufficient amount of that money is available to promote the economic growth of the nation.

Unfortunately for the unsuspecting public, that is not the case in any nation that is part of the international central bank system. That is because these are private institutions with shareholders to whom they owe accountability. That includes the Federal Reserve Bank the Central Bank of the United States, the banks that set the standard for the world to follow,

To understand what really happened, a brief history of the modern banking system is necessary.

Corbett (2014) insists that the story really began in late 17th century Europe, 1694 to be exact, as England was approaching the end of a 59 year war with France. King William III had endured a stunning naval defeat and had commit ted the court to rebuilding the English navy. But he was out of money as the government's coffers had been exhausted by the waging of the war. The king was also out of credit.

A Scottish banker by the name of William Paterson suggests to the king the formation of a company that would lend a million pounds to the Government at six percent plus a £5,000 'management fee. The agreement also included the right to issue notes in perpetuity.

The idea was accepted, and with it the Bank of England was created. The name of course is a carefully constructed lie, designed to make the bank appear to be a government entity. But it is not. It is a private bank owned by private shareholders for their private profit with a charter from the king that allows them to print the public's money out of thin air and lend it to the crown. What happens here at the birth of the Bank of England in 1694 is the creation of a template that will be repeated in country after country around the world: a privately controlled central bank lending money to the government at interest, money that it prints out of nothing. And the jewel in the crown for the international bankers that creates this system is the future economic power-house of the world, the United States. They knew that applying this model to the newly created colonies would be a bonanza for them.

In many important respects, the history of the United States is the history of the struggle of the American people against the bankers that wish to control their money, but in 1780 the newly formed nation was still at war against their previous colonial masters. In other words, despite a declaration of independence the United Kingdom was determined to bring their most valuable colony back under their control.

In 1781 the newly independent nation had been employing a currency known as The Continental, the paper currency issued by the Continental Congress to pay for the war debt, but thanks to an over issuing of the currency and British counterfeiting, the value to The Continental had collapsed. Desperate to find a way to finance the end stages of the war, Congress turns to Robert Morris, a wealthy shipping merchant who had been investigated for war profiteering just two years earlier. Now, as "Superintendent of Finance" of the United States from 1781 to 1784, he is regarded as the most powerful man in America next to General

Washington. In his capacity as Superintendent of Finance, Morris argues for the creation of a privately-owned central bank deliberately modeled on the Bank of England that the colonies were supposedly fighting against. Congress, backed into a corner by war obligations and forced to do business with the bankers just like King William in the 1690s, acquiesced and granted a charter for the Bank of North America, the nation's first central bank. Just as the Bank of England came into existence loaning the British crown 1.2 million pounds, the Bank of North America's first order of business was lending money to the congress at interest. The first sum that was printed and loaned to the congress was 1.2 million dollars. By the end of the war however, Morris has fallen out of political favor and the Bank of North America's currency had failed to win over a skeptical public. The Bank of North America was downgraded from a national central bank to a private commercial bank chartered by the State of Pennsylvania. But the bankers had no intentions of stopping there.

Before the ink is even dry on the Constitution, a group led by Alexander Hamilton was already working on the next privately-owned central bank for the newly formed, and so brazen was Hamilton in the forwarding of this central bank agenda that he makes no attempt to hide his aims or the aims of those of the banking interests he served. In a letter to James Duane in 1781 he wrote: "A national debt, if it is not excessive, will be to us a national blessing, it will be a powerful cement of our Union. It will also create a necessity for keeping up taxation to a degree which, without being oppressive, will be a spur to industry." Opposition to Hamilton and his debt-based system for establishing the finances of the US was fierce. That opposition was led by

Thomas Jefferson and James Madison, the bankers and their system of debt-enslavement is called out for the force of destruction that it is. As Thomas Jefferson wrote: "…The modern theory of the perpetuation of debt, has drenched the earth with blood, and crushed its inhabitants under burdens ever accumulating."

Debt is always crushing, it is the cause of many suicides, yet, in the mind of Hamilton, it is a good thing. In he mind of the banks and banking institutions that control the world, it is a good thing. Humans can function without massive debt. Trade and industry do not require crushing debt. This happens only in the minds of the vilest among us. Still, Hamilton proved victorious. The First Bank of the United States is chartered in 1791 and it followed the pattern of the Bank of England and the Bank of North America almost exactly; a privately-owned central bank with the authority to loan money that it creates out of nothing to the government. In fact, it is the very same people behind the new bank as those behind the old Bank of North America. It was Alexander Hamilton, Robert Morris' former aide, who first proposed Morris for the position of Financial Superintendent, and the director of the old Bank of North America, Thomas Willing, is brought in to serve as the first director of the First Bank of the United States. These were the first banking bosses of the newly created United States od America. In the first five years of the bank's existence, the US government borrowed 8.2 million dollars from the bank and prices rose 72%. By 1795, when Hamilton leaves office, the incoming Treasury Secretary announces that the government needs even more money and sells off the government's meager 20% share in the bank, making it a fully private corporation. Once again, the US economy is plundered while the private banking cartel laughs all the way to the bank that they created. By the time the bank's charter comes due for renewal in 1811, the tide has changed for the money interests behind the bank. Hamilton is dead, shot to death in a duel with Aaron Burr. The bank-supporting Federalist Party is out of power. The public are wary of foreign ownership of the central bank, and what's more don't see the point of a central bank in time of peace. Accordingly, the charter renewal is voted down in the Senate and the bank is closed in 1811.

But less than a year later, the US is once again at war with England, and after two years of bitter struggle, the public debt of the US has nearly tripled, from $45.2 million to $119.2 million. With trade at a standstill, prices soaring, inflation rising and debt mounting, President Madison signs the charter for the creation of another central bank, the Second Bank of the United States, in 1816.

Just like the two central banks before it, it is majority privately-owned and is granted the power to loan money that it creates out of thin air to the government. The 20-year bank charter is due to expire in 1836, but President Jackson has already vowed to let it die prior to renewal. Believing that Jackson won't risk his chance for reelection in 1832 on the issue, the bankers forward a bill to renew the bank's charter in July of that year, four years ahead of schedule. Remarkably, Jackson vetoes the renewal charter and stakes his reelection on the people's support of his move. In his veto message, Jackson writes in no uncertain terms about his opposition to the bank:

> Whatever interest or influence, whether public or private, has given birth to this act, it cannot be found either in the

wishes or necessities of the executive department, by which present action is deemed premature, and the powers conferred upon its agent not only unnecessary, but dangerous to the Government and country.

It is to be regretted that the rich and powerful too often bend the acts of government to their selfish purposes. If we cannot at once, in justice to interests vested under improvident legislation, make our Government what it ought to be, we can at least take a stand against all new grants of monopolies and exclusive privileges, against any prostitution of our Government to the advancement of the few at the expense of the many, and in favor of compromise and gradual reform in our code of laws and system of political economy.

The people sided with Jackson and he was reelected on the back of his slogan, "Jackson and No Bank!" The President makes good on his pledge. In 1833 he announces that the government will stop using the bank and will pay off its debt. The bankers retaliate in 1834 by staging a financial crisis and attempting to pin the blame on Jackson, but it's no use. On January 8, 1835, President Jackson succeeds in paying off the debt, and for the first and only time in its history the United States is free from the debt chain of the bankers. In 1836 the Second Bank of the United States' charter expires and the bank loses its status as America's central bank.

It took 77 years before the bankers could once again manipulate their way back into controlling the country's finances. But it is not for lack of trying. Immediately after Jackson killed the private banks, the banking oligarchs in England reacted by contracting trade, removing capital from the US, demanding payment in hard currency for all exports, and tightening credit. This resulted in a financial crisis known as the Panic of 1837.

For the remainder of the 1800s, the United States was rocked by banking panics brought on by wild banking speculation and sharp contractions in credit, so by 1900 the bulk of the money in the American economy had been centralized in the hands of a small clique of industrial magnates, each with a near-monopoly on a sector of the economy. These were the Astors in real estate; the Carnegies and the Schwabs in steel; the Harrimans, Stanfords and Vanderbilts in railroads; the Mellons and the Rockefellers in oil. As all of these families started to consolidate their fortunes, they gravitate naturally to the banking sector. And in this capacity, they form a network of financial interests and institutions that centered largely around one man, John Pierpont Morgan, banking scion and increasingly America's informal central banker in the absence of a central bank.

J P Morgan, or "Pierpont," as he prefers to be called, is born in Hartford, Connecticut, in 1837 to Junius Spencer Morgan, a successful banker and financier. Morgan rides his father's coat-tails into the banking business and by 1871 is partnered in his own firm, the firm that was eventually to become J.P. Morgan and Company.

It is Morgan who finances Cornelius Vanderbilt's New York Central Railroad. It is Morgan who finances the launch of nearly every major corporation of the period, from AT&T to General Electric to General Motors to DuPont. It is Morgan who buys out

Carnegie and creates the United States Steel Corporation, America's first billion-dollar company. It is Morgan who brokers a deal with President Grover Cleveland to "save" the nation's gold reserves by selling 62 million dollars' worth of gold to the Treasury in return for government bonds. And it is Morgan who, in 1907, sets in motion the crisis that leads to the creation of the Federal Reserve. That year, Morgan begins spreading rumors about the precarious finances of the Knickerbocker Trust Company, a Morgan competitor and one of the largest financial institutions in the United States at the time. The resulting crisis, dubbed the Panic of 1907, shakes the US financial system to its core. Morgan puts himself forward as a hero, boldly offering to help underwrite some of the faltering banks and brokerage houses to keep them from going under. After a bout of hand-wringing over the nation's finances, a Congressional Committee is assembled to investigate the "money trust," the bankers and financiers who brought the nation so close to financial ruin and who wield such power over the nation's finances. The public follows the issue closely, and in the end a handful of bankers are identified as key players in the money trust's operations, including Paul Warburg, Benjamin Strong, Jr., and J.P. Morgan.

According to Andrew Gavin Marshall, editor of The People's Book Project: "At the beginning of the 20th century there was an investigation following the greatest of these financial panics, which was in 1907, and this investigation was on *the money trust*." It found that three banking interests–J.P. Morgan, National City Bank, and the City Bank of New York–basically controlled the entire financial system.

The public hatred toward these institutions was unprecedented but the need for stabilization was eminent. The nation needed a fiduciary body that could control its finances. As a result, there was an overwhelming consensus in the country for establishing a central controlling bank. With the exception of the bankers everyone wanted government control of the central bank. They wanted it to be exclusively under the public control because they despised and feared the New York banks as wielding too much influence. So for them a central bank would be a way to curb the power of these private financial interests. On the other hand, those same financial interests were advocating for a central bank to serve as a source of stability for their control of the system, and also to act as a lender of last resort to them so they would never have to face collapse.

Unfortunately, the group that wielded more influence turned out to be the New York financial houses which were more aligned with the European financial houses than they were with any other element in American society, and so in a most dramatic conspiratorial scheme, they were able to manipulate the politicians into doing their biddings.

The plot began under the cover of darkness on 22 of November in 1910. That night a group of the richest and most powerful men in America were boarding a private rail car at an unassuming railroad station in Hoboken, New Jersey. The car, waiting with shades drawn to keep onlookers from seeing inside, belonged to Senator Nelson Aldrich, the father-in-law of billionaire heir to the Rockefeller dynasty, John D. Rockefeller, Jr. A central figure on the influential Senate Finance Committee, where he oversaw the nation's monetary policy, Aldrich was referred to in the press as the "General Manager of the Nation." Joining him that evening was his private secretary, Shelton, and a who's who of the nation's banking and financial elite: A. Piatt Andrew, the Assistant Treasury Secretary; Frank Vanderlip, President of the National City Bank of New York; Henry P. Davison, a senior partner of J.P. Morgan Company; Benjamin Strong, Jr., an associate of J.P. Morgan and President of Bankers Trust Co., and Paul Warburg, heir of the Warburg banking family and son-in-law of Solomon Loeb of the famed New York investment firm, Kuhn, Loeb & Company.

The men had been told to arrive one by one after sunset to attract as little attention as possible. Indeed, secrecy was so important to their mission that the group did not use anything but their first names throughout the journey so as to keep their true identities secret even from their own servants and wait staff. The movements of any one of them would have been reason enough to attract the attention of New York's voracious press, especially in an era where banking and monetary reform was seen as a key issue for the future of the nation; a meeting of all of them, now *that* would surely have been the story of the century. And it was. Their destination? The secluded Jekyll Island off the coast of Georgia, home to the prestigious Jekyll Island Club, whose members included the Morgans, Rockefellers, Warburgs, and Rothschilds. Their purpose? Davison told intrepid local newspaper reporters who had caught wind of the meeting that they were going duck hunting. But in reality, they were going to draft a reform of the nation's banking industry in complete secrecy.

G. Edward Griffin, the author of the best-selling The Creature from Jekyll Island and a long-time Federal Reserve researcher, explains:

> What happened is the banks decided that since there was going to be legislation anyway to control their industry, that they wouldn't just sit back and wait and see what happened and cross their fingers that it would be OK. They decided to do what so many cartels do today: they decided to take the lead. And they would be the ones calling for regulations and reform. They like the word *reform*.

The American people are suckers for that word. Put it into any corrupt piece of legislation and the invariably fall for it.

And so the banking cartel wrote their own rules and regulations, called it "The Federal Reserve Act," got it passed into law, and it was very much to their liking because they wrote it. In essence what they had created was a set of rules that made it possible for them to regulate their own industry, but they went even beyond that. Never in their wildest dream would they have expected that Congress would go along and also give them the right to issue the nation's money supply. So not only were they now going to regulate their own industry, but they got this incredible gift that they didn't dream would be given to them. Congress gave away the sovereign right to issue the nation's money to the private banks. All of this was stipulated in *The Federal Reserve Act*. Not only did they succeed in conspiring to write the legislation that would eventually become the Federal Reserve Act, they also succeeded in keeping that conspiracy a secret from the public for decades.

In an interesting display of high-level manipulation, the bankers pretended to protest against the legislation they introduced to the congress by writing articles that said the act would kill the banks. Even though they wrote the bill. The unsuspecting public read the articles and concluded that if the bankers did not like the Act it must be a good thing. It was all a gimmick, but it worked.

The first report on this malevolent act came about in 1916 by Bertie Charles Forbes, the financial writer who would later go on to found *Forbes* magazine. But none of the conspirators fully admitted to what had taken place. It wasn't until a full quarter-century later, when Frank Vanderlip wrote a casual admission of the meeting in the February 9, 1935, edition of *The Saturday Evening Post*. "I was as secretive—indeed, as furtive—as any conspirator. Do not feel it is any exaggeration to speak of our secret expedition to Jekyll Island as the occasion of the actual conception of what eventually became the Federal Reserve System." Over the course of their nine days of deliberation at the Jekyll Island Club, they devised a plan so overarching, so ambitious, that even they could scarcely imagine that it would ever be passed by Congress. As Vanderlip put it, "Discovery [of our plan], we knew, simply must not happen, or else all our time and effort would be wasted. If it were to be exposed publicly that our particular group had got together and written a banking bill, that bill would have no chance whatever of passage by Congress."

So, what precisely did this conclave of conspirators devise at their Jekyll Island meeting?

In essence a plan for a central banking system to be owned by the banks themselves, a system which would organize the nation's banks into a private cartel that would have sole control over the money supply itself. At the end of their nine-day meeting, the bankers and financiers went back to their respective offices content in what they had accomplished. The details of the plan changed between its 1910 drafting and the eventual passage of the Federal Reserve Act, but the essential ideas were there.

To achieve [its] goals, the Fed, then and now, combines centralized national authority through the Board of Governors with a healthy dose of regional independence through the reserve banks. A third entity, the Federal Open Market Committee, brings together the first two in setting the nation's monetary policy. The simple truth, hidden behind the sleight of hand of economic jargon and magisterial titles, is that a banking cartel has monopolized the most important item in our entire economy: money itself.

It should be pointed out that the main individual behind the founding of the Federal Reserve was Paul Warburg, who was a partner with Kuhn, Loeb and Company, a European banking house. His brothers were prominent bankers in Germany at that time, and he had of course close connections with every major financial and industrial firm in the United States and most of those existing in Europe. He was discussing all of these ideas with his fellow compatriots in advocating for a central bank. It was he who got the support of a Senator Aldrich in 1910, and persuaded him to organize the secret meeting in Georgia.

In his first attempt to present the plan to the U.S. Congress the public, suspicious of Senator Aldrich's banking connections, ultimately reject it. But they did not give up. They revised and rename their plan, giving it a new public face. This time they allowed it to be presented by Representative Carter Glass and Senator Robert Owen.

In the end, the money trust that was behind the Panic of 1907 uses the public's own outrage against them to complete their consolidation of control over the banking system. The newly retitled Federal Reserve Act is signed into law on December 23, 1913, and the Fed begins operations the next year.

Seven decades later the chairman of the Federal Reserve *Alan Greenspan* made a statement that reflects the extraordinary and perpetual powers of the Federal Reserve: "The Federal Reserve is an independent agency. That means no government agency can overrule the actions that we take."

The US dollar has been the reserve currency of the world since the end of World War 2, this means that all central banks hold US dollars in their reserve. In other words, all currencies must be backed by the US dollar. This links all currencies to the Federal Reserve monetary policies in America.

THE REAL STORY BEHIND WWI

The Canadian James Corbett of the *Corbett Report*, tells a story of WWI that many scholars and informed persons had not heard of. What is interesting is that Corbett asks his readers to reproduce and disseminate his research all in the interest of the public good. We took the liberty of reproducing that story here simply because this information is not available elsewhere. The reader can decide if the information is too conspiratorial to be credible, but the fact is that it must be presented. I've spent countless hours studying that war starting with high school. It was not until I watched the Corbett's report on that war that the entire story began to make sense.

Given the role Cecil Rhodes played in the development of that war I urge the reader to explore the life of Cecil Rhodes. There is a five-part biography on the complex life of a personality that so deeply impacted the 20th century, and it is available on you tube.

The story is of a happy gregarious young man who traveled to southern Africa to join his older brother as he prospected for gold and diamond on that continent. He was of ill health and his parents felt the weather in southern Africa would do him good. When he failed in this venture, Rhodes returned home to complete his education at Oxford University. There is where he became drunk with the indoctrination of Anglo-Saxon superiority over all other races and groups. Rhodes returned to southern Africa imbued with that sense of power and in no time, he was able to corner the diamond market becoming extremely wealthy with that trade before the age of 50. His racism, his vitriol and his ruthlessness especially with the native Africans was notorious.

His lifetime illnesses caught up with him and he died at the age of 52, but not before leaving his wealth to be administered by the Rothschilds in the form of an endowment to educate those who subscribe the ideas he held so dearly. Plenty of Rhode scholars abound today with a great deal of pride in their accomplishment. They wear their title as Rhode scholars as a badge of honor. I' not quite sure how many have taken the time to explore the life of their benefactor.

Like the religious mythologies, that war demonstrated more than anything else the vulnerability of the masses, and their willingness to work against their own best interests.

In Corbett's own words

November 11, 1918.

> All across the Western front, the clocks that were lucky enough to escape the four years of shelling chimed the eleventh hour. And with that the First World War came to an end.
>
> From 10 o'clock to 11 — the hour for the cessation of hostilities — the opposed batteries simply raised hell. Not even the artillery prelude to our advance into the Argonne had anything on it. To attempt an advance was out of the question. It was not a barrage. It was a deluge.
>
> Nothing quite electrical in effect as the sudden stop that came at 11 A. M. has ever occurred to me. It was 10:60 precisely and — the roar stopped like a motor car hitting a wall. The resulting quiet was uncanny in comparison. From somewhere far below ground,

Germans began to appear. They clambered to the parapets and began to shout wildly. They threw their rifles, hats, bandoleers, bayonets and trench knives toward us. They began to sing.

And just like that, it was over. Four years of the bloodiest carnage the world had ever seen came to a stop as sudden and bewildering as its start. And the world vowed "Never again."

Each year, we lay the wreath. We hear "The Last Post." We mouth the words "never again" like an incantation. But what does it *mean*? To answer this question, we have to understand what WWI *was*.

WWI was an explosion, a breaking point in history. In the smoldering shell hole of that great cataclysm lay the industrial-era optimism of never-ending progress. Old verities about the glory of war lay strewn around the battlefields of that "Great War" like a fallen soldier left to die in No Man's Land, and along with it lay all the broken dreams of a world order that had been blown apart. Whether we know it or not, we here in the 21st century, are still living in the crater of that explosion, the victims of a First World War that we are only now beginning to understand. What was World War One about? How did it start? Who won? And what did they win? Now, 100 years after those final shots rang out, these questions still puzzle historians and laymen alike. But as we shall see, this confusion is not a happenstance of history but the wool that has been pulled over our eyes to stop us from seeing what WWI really was.

This is the story of WWI that you didn't read in the history books.

This is **The WWI Conspiracy**.

PART ONE – TO START A WAR

June 28, 1914.

The Archduke Franz Ferdinand, heir to the Austro-Hungarian throne, and his wife Sophie are in Sarajevo for a military inspection. In retrospect, it's a risky provocation, like tossing a match into a powder keg. Serbian nationalism is rising, the Balkans are in a tumult of diplomatic crises and regional wars, and tensions between the kingdom of Serbia and the Austro-Hungarian Empire are set to spill over.

But despite warnings and ill omens, the royal couple's security is extremely lax. They board an open-top sports car and proceed in a six-car motorcade along a pre-announced route. After an inspection of the military barracks, they head toward the Town Hall for a scheduled reception by the Mayor. The visit is going ahead exactly as planned and precisely on schedule.

And then the bomb goes off.

As we now know, the motorcade was a death trap. Six assassins lined the royal couple's route that morning, armed with bombs and pistols. The first two failed to act, but the third, Nedeljko Čabrinović, panicked and threw his bomb onto the folded back cover of the Archduke's convertible. It bounced off onto the street, exploding under the next car in the convoy. Franz Ferdinand and his wife, unscathed, were rushed on to the Town Hall, passing the other assassins along the route too quickly for them to act. Having narrowly escaped death, the Archduke called off the rest of his scheduled itinerary to visit the wounded from the bombing at the hospital. By a remarkable twist of fate, the driver took the couple down the wrong route, and, when ordered to reverse, stopped the car directly in front of the delicatessen where would-be assassin Gavrilo Princip had gone after having failing in his mission along the motorcade. There, one and a half meters in front of Princip, were the Archduke and his wife. He took two shots, killing both of them.

Yes, even the official history books—the books written and published by the "winners"—record that the First World War started as the result of a conspiracy. After all, it was—as all freshman history students are taught—the conspiracy to assassinate the Archduke Franz Ferdinand that led to the outbreak of war.

That story, the official story of the origins of World War I, is familiar enough by now: In 1914, Europe was an interlocking clockwork of alliances and military mobilization plans that, once set in motion, ticked inevitably toward all out warfare. The assassination of the Archduke was merely the excuse to set that clockwork in motion, and the resulting "July crisis" of diplomatic and military escalations led with perfect predictability to continental and, eventually, global war. In this carefully sanitized version of history, World War I starts in Sarajevo on June 28, 1914.

But this official history leaves out so much of the real story about the build up to war that it amounts to a lie. But it does get one thing right: The First World War *was* the result of a conspiracy.

To understand this conspiracy we must turn not to Sarajevo and the conclave of Serbian nationalists plotting their assassination in the summer of 1914, but to a chilly drawing room in London in the winter of 1891. There, three of the most important men of the age—men whose names are but dimly remembered today—are taking the first concrete steps toward forming a secret society that they have been discussing amongst themselves for years. The group that springs from this meeting will go on to leverage the wealth and power of its members to shape the course of history and, 23 years later, will drive the world into the first truly global war.

Their plan reads like outlandish historical fiction. They will form a secret organization dedicated to the "extension of British rule throughout the world" and "the ultimate recovery of the United States of America as an integral part of a British Empire." The group is to be structured along the lines of a religious brotherhood (the Jesuit order is repeatedly invoked as a model) divided into two circles: an inner circle, called "The Society of the Elect," who are to direct the activity of the larger, outer circle, dubbed "The Association of Helpers" who are not to know of the inner circle's existence.

"British rule" and "inner circles" and "secret societies." If presented with this plan today, many would say it was the work of an imaginative comic book writer. But the three men who gathered in London that winter afternoon in 1891 were no mere comic book writers; they were among the wealthiest and most influential men in British society, and they had access to the resources and the contacts to make that dream into a reality.

Present at the meeting that day: William T. Stead, famed newspaper editor whose *Pall Mall Gazette* broke ground as a pioneer of tabloid journalism and whose *Review of Reviews* was enormously influential throughout the English-speaking world; Reginald Brett, later known as Lord Esher, an historian and politician who became friend, confidant and advisor to Queen Victoria, King Edward VII, and King George V, and who was known as one of the primary powers-behind-the-throne of his era; and Cecil Rhodes, the enormously wealthy diamond magnate whose exploits in South Africa and ambition to transform the African continent would earn him the nickname of "Colossus" by the satirists of the day.

But Rhodes' ambition was no laughing matter. If anyone in the world had the power and ability to form such a group at the time, it was Cecil Rhodes.

Cecil Rhodes also was from Britain. He was educated at Oxford, but he only went to Oxford after he went to South Africa. He had an older brother he follows into South Africa. The older brother was working in the diamond mines, and by the time Rhodes gets there he's got a set up, and his brother says "I'm going to go off and dig in the gold mines. They just found gold!" And so he leaves Cecil Rhodes, his younger brother—who's, like, in his 20s—with this whole diamond mining operation. Rhodes then goes to Oxford, comes back down to South Africa with the help of Lord Rothschild, who had funding efforts behind De Beers and taking advantage of that situation. And from there they began to use "slave labor," which eventually was transformed into the *apartheid* policy of South Africa.

And in fact that was centered in a very secretive place called "All Souls College." Still you'll find many references to All Souls College and "people behind the curtain" and such phrases [as] "power behind thrones." Rhodes was centrally important in actually putting money up in order to begin to bring together like-minded people of great influence.

Rhodes was not shy about his ambitions, and his intentions to form such a group were known to many.

Throughout his short life, Rhodes discussed his intentions openly with many of his associates, who, unsurprisingly, happened to be among the most influential figures in British society at that time.

More remarkably, this secret society—which was to wield its power behind the throne—was not a secret at all. *The New York Times* even published an article discussing the founding of the group in the April 9, 1902, edition of the paper, shortly after Rhodes' death.

The article, headlined "Mr. Rhodes's Ideal of Anglo-Saxon Greatness" and carrying the remarkable sub-head "He Believed a Wealthy Secret Society Should Work to Secure the World's Peace and a British-American Federation," summarized this sensational plan by noting that Rhodes' "idea for the development of the English-speaking race was the foundation of 'a society copied, as to organization, from the Jesuits.'" Noting that his vision involved uniting "the United States Assembly and our House of Commons to achieve 'the peace of the world,'" the article quotes Rhodes as saying: "The only thing feasible to carry out this idea is a secret society gradually absorbing the wealth of the world."

This idea is laid down in black and white in a series of wills that Rhodes wrote throughout his life, wills that not only laid out his plan to create such a society and provided the funds to do so, but, even more re-markably, were collected in a volume published after his death by co-conspirator William T. Stead.

Not ever marrying and not having any children, Rhodes left the Rothschilds as executors of his will before dying at the young age of 52 in 1902.

There's a book published that contains his last will and testament. The guy who wrote the book, William T. Stead, was in charge of a British publication called *The Review of Reviews*. He was part of Rhodes' Round Table group. He at one time was an executor for the will, and in that will it says that he laments the loss of America from the British Empire and that they should formulate a secret society with the specific aim of bringing America back into the Empire. Then he names all the countries that they need to include in this list to have world domination, to have an English-speaking union, to have British race as the enforced culture on all countries around the world.

The will contains the goal. The goal is amended over a series of years and supported and used to gain support. And then, by the time he dies in 1902, there's funding, there's a plan, there's an agenda, there's working groups, and it all launches and then takes hold. And then not too long later, you've got World War One and then from that you've got World War Two and then you've got a century of control and slavery that really could have been prevented.

When, at the time of Rhodes' death in 1902, this "secret" society decided to partially reveal itself, it did so under the cloak of peace. It was only because they desired world peace, they insisted, that they had created their group in the first place, and only for the noblest of reasons that they aimed to "gradually absorb the wealth of the world."

But contrary to this pacific public image, from its very beginnings the group was interested primarily in war. In fact, one of the very first steps taken by this "Rhodes Round Table" (as it was known by some) was to maneuver the British Empire into war in South Africa. This "Boer War" of 1899–1902 would serve a dual purpose: it would unite the disparate republics and colonies of South Africa into a single unit under British imperial control, and, not incidentally, it would bring the rich gold deposits of the Transvaal Republic into the orbit of the Rothschild/Rhodes-controlled British South Africa Company.

The war was, by the group's own admission, entirely its doing. The point man for the operation was Sir Alfred Milner, a close associate of Rhodes and a member of the secret society's inner circle who was then the governor of the British Cape Colony. Although largely forgotten today, Alfred Milner (later 1st Viscount Milner) was perhaps the most important single figure in Britain at the dawn of the

20th century. From Rhodes' death in 1902, he became the unofficial head of the roundtable group and directed its operations, leveraging the vast wealth and influence of the group's exclusive membership to his own ends.

With Milner, there was no compunction or moral hand-wringing about the methods used to bring about those ends. In a letter to Lord Roberts, Milner casually confessed to having engineered the Boer War: "I precipitated the crisis, which was inevitable, before it was too late. It is not very agreeable, and in many eyes, not a very creditable piece of business to have been largely instrumental in bringing about a war."

When Rhodes' co-conspirator and fellow secret society inner circle member William Stead objected to war in South Africa, Rhodes told him: "You will support Milner in any measure that he may take short of war. I make no such limitation. I support Milner absolutely without reserve. If he says peace, I say peace; if he says war, I say war. Whatever happens, I say ditto to Milner."

The Boer War, involving unimaginable brutality— including the death of 26,000 women and children in the world's first (British) concentration camps— ended as Rhodes and his associates intended: with the formerly separate pieces of South Africa being united under British control. Perhaps even more importantly from the perspective of the secret society, it left Alfred Milner as High Commission of the new South African Civil Service, a position from which he would cultivate a team of bright, young, largely Oxford-educated men who would go on to serve the group and its ends.

And from the end of the Boer War onward, those ends increasingly centered on the task of eliminating what Milner and the Round Table perceived as the single greatest threat to the British Empire: Germany.

At the outset it was about influencing people who could influence politics, people who had the money to influence statesmen, and the dream. The dream of actually crushing Germany. This was a basic mindset of this group as it got together.

In 1871, the formerly separate states of modern-day Germany united into a single empire under the rule of Wilhelm I. The consolidation and industrialization of a united Germany had fundamentally changed the balance of power in Europe. By the dawn of the 20th century, the British Empire found itself dealing not with its traditional French enemies or its long-standing Russian rivals for supremacy over Europe, but the upstart German Empire. Economically, technologically, even militarily; if the trends continued, it would not be long before Germany began to rival and even surpass the British Empire.

112

For Alfred Milner and the group, he had formed around him out of the old Rhodes Round Table society, it was obvious what had to be done: to change France and Russia from enemies into friends as a way of isolating, and, eventually, crushing Germany. Peter Hof, author of *The Two Edwards: How King Edward VII and Foreign Secretary Sir Edward Grey Fomented the First World War*, stated: Yes, well from the British perspective, Germany, after their unification in 1871, they became very strong very quickly. And over time this worried the British more and more, and they began to think that Germany represented a challenge to their world hegemony. And slowly but surely, they came to the decision that Germany must be confronted just as they had come to the same decision with regard to other countries—Spain and Portugal and especially France and now Germany.

German finished goods were marginally better than those of Britain, they were building ships that were marginally better than those of Britain, and all of this. The British elite very slowly came to the decision that Germany needed to be confronted while it was still possible to do so. It might not be possible to do so if they waited too long. And so this is how the decision crystallized.

I think that Britain might possibly have accepted the German ascendance, but they had something that was close at hand, and that was the Franco-Russian

Alliance. And they thought if they could hook in with that alliance, then they had the possibility of defeating Germany quickly and without too much trouble. And that is basically what they did.

But crafting an alliance with two of Britain's biggest rivals and turning public opinion against one of its dearest continental friends was no mean feat. To do so would require nothing less than for Milner and his group to seize control of the press, the military and all the diplomatic machinery of the British Empire. And so that's exactly what they did.

The first major coup occurred in 1899, while Milner was still in South Africa launching the Boer War. That year, the Milner Group ousted Donald Mackenzie Wallace, the director of the foreign department at *The Times*, and installed their man, Ignatius Valentine Chirol. Chirol, a former employee of the Foreign Office with inside access to officials there, not only helped to ensure that one of the most influential press organs of the Empire would spin all international events for the benefit of the secret society, but he helped to prepare his close personal friend, Charles Hardinge, to take on the crucial post of Ambassador to Russia in 1904, and, in 1906, the even more important post of Permanent Under-Secretary at the Foreign Office.

With Hardinge, Milner's Group had a foot in the door at the British Foreign Office. But they needed more than just their foot in that door if they were to

bring about their war with Germany. In order to fin-
ish the coup, they needed to install one of their own
as Foreign Secretary. And, with the appointment of
Edward Grey as Foreign Secretary in December of
1905, that's precisely what happened.

Sir Edward Grey was a valuable and trusted ally of
the Milner Group. He shared their anti-German sentiment and, in his important position of Foreign Secretary, showed no compunction at all about using
secret agreements and unacknowledged alliances to
further set the stage for war with Germany. He became foreign secretary in 1905, and the foreign secretary in France was of course Delcassé. And
Delcassé was equally anti-German and passionate
about the recovery of Alsace-Lorraine, and so he and
the king hit it off very well together. And Edward
Grey shared this anti-German feeling with the
king—as I explained in my book how he came to
have that attitude about Germany. But in any case,
he had the same attitude with the king. They worked
very well together. Edward Grey very freely
acknowledged the heavy role that the king played in
British foreign policy and he said that this was not a
problem because he and the king were in agreement
on most issues and so they worked with very well together.

The pieces were already beginning to fall into place
for Milner and his associates. With Edward Grey as

foreign secretary, Hardinge as his unusually influential undersecretary, Rhodes' co-conspirator Lord Esher installed as deputy governor of Windsor Castle where he had the ear of the king, and the king himself—whose unusual, hands-on approach to foreign diplomacy and whose wife's own hatred of the Germans dovetailed perfectly with the group's aims—the diplomatic stage was set for the formation of the Triple Entente between France, Russia and Great Britain. With France to the west and Russia to the east, England's secret diplomacy had forged the two pincers of a German-crushing vise.

All that was needed was an event that the group could spin to its advantage to prepare the population for war against their former German allies. Time and again throughout the decade leading up to the "Great War," the group's influential agents in the British press tried to turn every international incident into another example of German hostility.

When the Russo-Japanese War broke out, rumors swirled in London that it was in fact the Germans that had stirred up the hostilities. The theory went that Germany—in a bid to ignite conflict between Russia and England, who had recently concluded an alliance with the Japanese—had fanned the flames of war between Russia and Japan. The truth, of course, was almost precisely the opposite. Lord Lansdowne had conducted secret negotiations with Japan before signing a formal treaty in January

1902. Having exhausted their reserves building up their military, Japan turned to Cecil Rhodes' co-conspirator Lord Nathan Rothschild to finance the war itself. Denying the Russian navy access to the Suez Canal and high-quality coal, which they *did* provide to the Japanese, the British did everything they could to ensure that the Japanese would crush the Russian fleet, effectively removing their main European competitor for the Far East. The Japanese navy was even constructed in Britain, but these facts did not find their way into the Milner-controlled press.

When the Russians "accidentally" fired on British fishing trawlers in the North Sea in 1904, killing three fishermen and wounding several more, the British public was outraged. Rather than whip up the outrage, however, *The Times* and other mouthpieces of the secret society instead tried to paper over the incident. Meanwhile, the British Foreign Office outrageously tried to blame the incident on the Germans, kicking off a bitter press war between Britain and Germany.

The most dangerous provocations of the period centered around Morocco, when France—emboldened by secret military assurances from the British and backed up by the British press—engaged in a series of provocations, repeatedly breaking assurances to Germany that Morocco would remain free and open to German trade. At each step, Milner's acolytes, both in government and in the British press, cheered

on the French and demonized any and every response from the Germans, real or imagined.

On May 7, 1915 "Colonel" Edward Mandell House
met with King George V, who had ascended to the
throne after the death Edward VII's in 1910. Accompanying him is Edward Grey, British foreign secretary and acolyte of the Milner Group. The two speak
"of the probability of an ocean liner being sunk" and
House informs Grey that "if this were done, a flame
of indignation would sweep across America, which
would in itself probably carry us into the war."

An hour later, at Buckingham Palace, King George V
inquiries about an even more specific event.

They discussed the probability of Germany sinking
a trans-Atlantic liner with American passengers on
board, more specifically, the *Lusitania*.

Coincidently, at 2:00 that afternoon, just hours after
these conversations took place, that is precisely
what happened.

The *Lusitania*, one of the largest passenger liners in
the world, was en route from New York to Liverpool
when it is struck by a torpedo from a German U-
boat. She sinks to the bottom in minutes, killing
1,198 passengers and crew, including 128 Americans. The disaster—portrayed as a brazen, unex-
pected attack on an innocent passenger liner—helps
to shift public opinion about the war in the US. To
the average American, the war suddenly doesn't feel
like a strictly European concern.

Every aspect of the story was, as we now know, a deception. The *Lusitania* was not an innocent passenger liner but an armed merchant cruiser officially listed by the British Admiralty as an auxiliary war ship. It was outfitted with extra armor, designed to carry twelve six-inch guns, and equipped with shell racks for holding ammunition. On its transatlantic voyage the ship was carrying "war materiel"—specifically, more than four million .303 rifle bullets and tons of munitions, including shells, powder, fuses and gun cotton—"in unrefrigerated cargo holds that were dubiously marked cheese, butter and oysters." This secret manifest was officially denied by the British government for generation after generation, but in 2014—a full 99 years after the event—internal government documents were finally released in which the government admitted the deception.

It was the secret society's multiyear campaign to draw the United States into World War I. But in order to understand this story, we have to meet Edward Mandell House and the other Milner Group co-conspirators in America.

Strange as it might seem, there was no shortage of such co-conspirators in the US. Some, like the members of the influential Pilgrim Society, founded in 1902 for the "encouragement of Anglo-American good fellowship"—shared Rhodes' vision of a united Anglo-American world empire; others were simply lured by the promise of money. But whatever their motivation, those sympathetic to the cause of the Round Table included some of the wealthiest and most powerful people in the United States at the time.

Many of these figures were to be found at the heart of Wall Street, in the banking and financial institutions revolving around J.P. Morgan and Company. John Pierpont Morgan, or "Pierpont" as he preferred to be called, was the nucleus of turn-of-the-century America's banking sector. Getting his start in London in 1857 at his father's merchant banking firm, the young Pierpont returned to New York in 1858 and embarked on one of the most remarkable careers in the history of the world.

Making his money financing the American robber barons of the late 19th century—from Vanderbilt's railroads to Adolph Simon Ochs' purchase of *The New York Times* to the buyout of Carnegie Steel—Morgan amassed a financial empire that, by the 1890s, wielded more power than the United States Treasury itself. He teamed up with his close allies, the House of Rothschild, to bail out the US government during a gold shortage in 1895 and eased the Panic of 1907 (which he helped to precipitate) by locking 120 of the country's most prestigious bankers in his library and forcing them to reach a deal on a $25 million loan to keep the banking system afloat.

As we saw in "Century of Enslavement: The History of the Federal Reserve," Morgan and his associates were only too happy to use the banking crises they helped to create to galvanize public opinion toward the creation of a central bank, so long as that central bank was owned and directed by Wall Street.

But their initial plan, the Aldrich Plan, was immediately recognized as a Wall Street ploy. Morgan and his fellow bankers were going to have to find a suitable cover to get their act through Congress, including, preferably, a President with sufficient progressive cover to give the new "Federal Reserve Act" an air of legitimacy. And they found their ideal candidate in the politically unknown President of Princeton University, Woodrow Wilson, a man who they were about to rocket straight into the White House with the help of their point man and Round Table co-conspirator, Edward Mandell House.

Woodrow Wilson was an obscure professor at Princeton University who apparently was not a very smart guy, but he was smart enough to pick up when other people had good ideas and then he bumps into this guy named Colonel House.

Colonel House, he grew up in Beaumont, Texas, and Colonel House's dad was like a Rhett Butler type of smuggler privateer pirate during the Confederate war with the Union. So, Colonel House: first of all, he's not a colonel. It's just like a title he gave himself to make him seem more than he was. But he did come from a politically connected family in the South that were doing business with the British during the Civil War. So Colonel House in the early 1900s makes Woodrow Wilson his protegé, and Colonel House himself is being puppeted by a few people in the layers of the Anglo-American establishment above him, and so we are left with the public persona of Woodrow Wilson. And here he is.

The election of Woodrow Wilson once again shows how power operates behind the scenes to subvert the popular vote and the will of the public. Knowing that the stuffy and politically unknown Wilson would have little chance of being elected over the more popular and affable William Howard Taft, Morgan and his banking allies bankrolled Teddy Roosevelt on a third party ticket to split the Republican vote. The strategy worked and the banker's real choice, Woodrow Wilson, came to power with just forty-two percent of the popular vote.

With Wilson in office and Colonel House directing his actions, Morgan and his conspirators get their wish. 1913 saw the passage of both the federal income tax and the Federal Reserve Act, thus consolidating Wall Street's control over the economy. World War One, brewing in Europe just eight months after the creation of the Federal Reserve, was to be the first full test of that power.

But difficult as it had been for the Round Table to coax the British Empire out of its "splendid isolation" from the continent and into the web of alliances that precipitated the war, it would be that much harder for their American fellow travelers to coax the United States out of its own isolationist stance. Although the Spanish-American War had seen the advent of American imperialism, the thought of the US getting involved in "that European war" was still far from the minds of the average American.

A 1914 editorial from *The New York Sun* captures the sentiment of most of America at the time of the outbreak of the war in Europe:

"There is nothing reasonable in such a war as that for which Europe has been making ready, and it would be folly for this country to sacrifice itself to the frenzy of dynastic policies and the clash of ancient hatreds which is urging the Old World to its destruction."

The Sun was by no means unique in its assessment. A vote taken among 367 newspapers throughout the United States in November of 1914 found just 105 pro-Ally and 20 pro-German papers, with the vast majority—242 of them—remaining firmly neutral and recommending that Uncle Sam stay out of the conflict.

Once again, just as they did in Britain, the cabal was going to have to leverage its control of the press and key governmental positions to begin to shape public perception and instill pro-war sentiment. And once again, the full resources of these motivated co-conspirators were brought to bear on the task.

One of the first shells in this barrage of propaganda to penetrate the American consciousness was the "Rape of Belgium," a catalogue of scarcely believable atrocities allegedly committed by the German forces in their invasion and occupation of Belgium at the start of the war. In a manner that was to become the norm in 20th century propaganda, the stories had a kernel of truth; there is no doubt that there were atrocities committed and civilians murdered by German forces in Belgium. But the propaganda that was spun from those kernels of truth was so over-the-top in its attempts to portray the Germans as inhuman brutes that it serves as a perfect example of war propaganda.

The American population at that time had a lot of German people in it. Thirty to fifty percent of the population had relations back to Germany, so there had to be this very clever propaganda campaign. It's known today as "babies on bayonets." So if you have no interest in World War I but you think it's interesting to study propaganda so you don't get fooled again, then type it into your favorite search engine: "babies on bayonets, World War I." You'll see hundreds of different posters where the Germans are bayonetting babies and it brings about emotions and it doesn't give you the details of anything. And emotions drive wars, not facts. Facts are left out and deleted all the time in order to create wars, so I think that putting facts back in might help prevent wars. But I do know that they like to drive people on emotion. The "babies on bayonets" getting America into World War I, that's a key part of it.

They made up stories of children who had their arms chopped off. Nuns that were raped. Shocking things, genuinely shocking things. The Canadian officer who was nailed at St. Andrew's cross on a church door and left there to bleed to death. These were the great myths peddled in order to defame and bring down the whole image of any justification for German action and try and influence America into war.

That's not to say that there weren't atrocities on both sides. War is an atrocious event, and there are always victims. Absolutely. And one can offer no justification for it. But the lies, the unnecessary abuse of propaganda.

The campaign had its intended effect. Horrified by the stories emerging from Belgium—stories picked up and amplified by the members of the Round Table in the British press, including the influential *Times* and the lurid *Daily Mail*, run by Milner ally Lord Northcliffe—American public opinion began to shift away from viewing the war as a European squabble about an assassinated archduke and toward viewing the war as a struggle against the evil Germans and their "sins against civilization."

The report itself, concluding that the Germans had systematically and premeditatedly broken the "rules and usages of war" was published on May 12, 1915, just five days after the sinking of *The Lusitania*. Directly between these two events, on May 9, 1915, Colonel House—the man whom Wilson called his "second personality" and his "independent self"— wrote a telegram, which the President dutifully read to his cabinet and was picked up by newspapers across the country.

"America has come to the parting of the ways, when she must determine whether she stands for civilized or uncivilized warfare. We can no longer remain neutral spectators. Our action in this crisis will determine the part we will play when peace is made, and how far we may influence a settlement for the lasting good of humanity. We are being weighed in the balance, and our position amongst nations is being assessed by mankind."

But despite this all-out propaganda assault, the American public was still largely against entering the war. It was in this context that the same group of Wall Street financiers who had maneuvered Wilson into the White House presided over the 1916 presidential election, one that the country knew would decisively conclude America's neutrality in the war or its decision to send forces to engage in European combat for the first time in history.

The bankers left nothing to chance. Wilson, who would predictably follow House's lead on all matters including war, was still their preferred candidate, but his competitor, Charles Evan Hughes, was no less of a Wall Street man. Hughes' roots were as a Wall Street lawyer; his firm represented the New York, Westchester, and Boston Railroad Company for J.P. Morgan and Company and the Baptist Bible class that he led boasted many wealthy and influential members, including John D. Rockefeller, Jr.

The affable Hughes was stiff competition for the wooden and charmless Wilson, but such was the importance of American neutrality that "He Kept Us out of War" actually became the central slogan of the campaign that saw Wilson return to the White House.

Towards the election of 1916 Wilson wasn't popular, but his propaganda for the election was "He Kept Us out of War." "He was a man, vote for Wilson, he kept us out of war." And then having promised that he would continue to keep America out of war, and in fact of course within months America was *thrown* into the war by its own government.

"He Kept Us Out of War." But just as in the British election of 1906—which saw the British public overwhelmingly voting for Henry Campbell-Bannerman's Liberal Party and their platform of peace only to get the Milnerites in the cabinet entering secret agreements to bring about war—so, too, was the American public duped at the ballot box in 1916.

In fact, in the fall of 1915, over one year before the election even took place, Wilson's string-puller, Edward Mandell House, was engaged in a secret negotiation with Edward Grey, the Milnerites heading Britain's foreign office. That negotiation—long hidden from the public but finally revealed when House's papers were published in 1928—shows the lengths to which Grey and House were willing to go to draw America into the war on the side of the Allies and against the Germans.

On October 17, 1915, House drafted a letter to Grey which he called "one of the most important letters I ever wrote." Before sending it, he split it into two separate, coded messages, to ensure it would not be readable if it were intercepted. In it, he laid out a plan to steer the US into war with Germany under the false pretense of a "peace conference."

Dear Sir Edward:

. . . In my opinion, it would be a world-wide calamity if the war should continue to a point where the Allies could not, with the aid of the United States, bring about a peace along the lines you and I have so often discussed.

It is in my mind that, after conferring with your Government, I should proceed to Berlin and tell them that it was the President's purpose to intervene and stop this destructive war, provided the weight of the United States thrown on the side that accepted our proposal could do it.

I would not let Berlin know, of course, of any understanding had with the Allies, but would rather lead them to think our proposal would be rejected by the Allies. This might induce Berlin to accept the proposal, but, if they did not do so, it would nevertheless be the purpose to intervene.

Perhaps realizing the gravity of what was being proposed, Woodrow Wilson, the man who would later be elected for his ability to keep America out of war, merely added the word "probably" to House's assurance that America would join the war.

The negotiations for this plan continued throughout the fall of 1915 and winter of 1916. In the end, the British government balked at the proposal because the thought that the Germans might actually accept peace—even a piece of disarmament brokered by the US—was not enough. They wanted to crush Germany completely and nothing less than total defeat would be sufficient. Another pretense would have to be manufactured to embroil the US in the war.

When, on the morning of May 7, 1915, House assured Grey and King George that the sinking of the *Lusitania* would cause "a flame of indignation [to] sweep across America," he was correct. When he said it would "probably carry us into war," he was mistaken. But in the end, it *was* the naval issue that eventually became the pretext for America's entry into war.

The history books of the period, following the familiar pattern of downplaying Allied provocations and focusing only on the German reactions, highlight the German policy of unrestricted submarine warfare which led to the downing of the *Lusitania*. The practice, which called for German U-boats to attack merchant ships on sight, was in contravention of the international rules of the sea at the time, and was widely abhorred as barbaric. But the policy was not instituted out of any insane blood lust on the part of the Kaiser; it was in response to Britain's own policy of breaking international rules of the sea.

At the outbreak of war in 1914, the British had used their position of naval superiority to begin a blockade of Germany. That campaign, described as "one of the largest and most complex undertakings attempted by either side during the First World War," involved the declaration of the whole of the North Sea as a war zone. As a so-called "distant blockade," involving the indiscriminate mining of an entire region of the high seas, the practice was in direct violation of the Declaration of Paris of 1856. The indiscriminate nature of the blockade—declaring the most basic of supplies, like cotton, and even food itself to be "contraband"—was a violation of the Declaration of London of 1909.

More to the point, as an attempt to starve an entire country into submission, it was a crime against humanity. Eventually reduced to a starvation diet of 1,000 calories a day, tuberculosis, rickets, edema and other maladies began to prey on those Germans who did not succumb to hunger. By the end of the war the National Health Office in Berlin calculated that 763,000 people had died as a direct result of the blockade. Perversely, the blockade did not end with the war. In fact, with Germany's Baltic coast now effectively added to the blockade, the starvation actually continued and even intensified into 1919.

Faced with protestations from the Austrian ambassador about the illegality of the British blockade, Colonel House, now America's de facto president, merely observed: "He forgets to add that England is not exercising her power in an objectionable way, for it is controlled by a democracy."

This double standard was not the exception but the rule when it came to those in America's East coast establishment, who were hungry to see the US join the Allies on the battlefields of Europe. As historian and author Ralph Raico explained in a 1983 lecture, it was these double standards that led directly to America's entry into the war. Raico (1983) The Wilson Administration took the position which lead ultimately to war and he made the German government accountable for the death of any Americans on the high seas regardless of circumstances.

The Germans were willing to live with these conditions as long as the Americans were willing to put pressure on the British to have them modify their violations of international law—that is, they're placing food on the list of contraband materials, which had never been done before. The British, as you know, take your merchant ships off the high seas on the way to Rotterdam because they say anything that goes to Rotterdam is going to go to Germany, so they take American ships off the high seas. The British have put cotton—cotton! —on the list of contraband, confiscating these materials. They interfere with letters going to the continent because they think there's military intelligence possibly involved. The British are imposing in many ways on Americans. So, if you hold them responsible, we'll behave ourselves as far as submarines go."

This was not to be the case, and the attitude of the Americans towards British violations of neutral rights were quite different. One reason is that the American ambassador to London, Walter Hines Page, was an extreme Anglophile. One time, for instance, he gets a message from the State Department saying, "Tell the British they have to stop interfering with American mail shipments to neutral ports. And the American ambassador goes to the British Foreign Minister Edward Grey and says, "Look at the message I've just got from Washington. Let's get together and try to answer this." This was his attitude.

The British were never held to the same standard as the Germans.

At home, Theodore Roosevelt, who in previous years had been a great friend of the Kaiser's and a great admirer of Germany, now says we have to get into this war right away. Besides that, there's a campaign for preparedness for building up the American Navy, drilling American citizens in combat techniques. There's a kind of hysteria, really, that travels over the country considering that there's—at this time, certainly—no chance, no chance of some kind of immediate threat to the United States.

And people like Roosevelt and Wilson begin talking in a very unfortunate way. Wilson says, for instance, "In America we have too many hyphenated Americans"—of course he meant German-Americans, Irish-Americans—"and these people are not totally loyal to our country." Already scapegoats are being looked for and public opinion is being roused.

And this diplomatic negotiation, the exchange of memos, goes on for the next few years. In January of 1917, the Americans, not having been able to budge the British in the least on any British violation of American rights; the British blockade intensifying; the Germans really feeling hunger in a very literal sense, especially the people on the on the home front; the Kaiser is persuaded by his Admirals and Generals to begin unrestricted submarine warfare around the British Isles.

The American position by this time had solidified, had become a totally rigid one, and when all is said and done, when you go through all of the back-and-forth memoranda and notes and principles established, the United States went to war against Germany in 1917 for the right of Americans to travel in armed belligerent merchant ships carrying munitions through war zones. Wilson's position was that even in that case the Germans simply had no right to attack the ship as long as there are Americans on the ship. Shall I repeat that? Armed belligerent—that is to say, English—armed English merchant ships carrying munitions could not be fired upon by the Germans as long as there were American citizens on board. And it was for the right of Americans to go into the war zone on such vessels that we finally went to war.

After months of deliberations and with the situation on the home front becoming increasingly desperate, the German military commanders decided to resume their unrestricted submarine warfare in 1917. As expected, US merchant ships were sunk, including four ships in late March alone. On April 2, 1917, Woodrow Wilson made his historic speech calling for Congress to declare war on Germany and commit US troops to European battlefields for the first time. The speech, made over one hundred years ago by and for a world that has long since passed away, still resonates with us today. Embedded within it is the rhetoric of warfare that has been employed by president after president, prime minister after prime minister, in country after country and war after war right down to the current day. From it comes many of the phrases that we still recognize today as the language of lofty ideals and noble causes that always accompany the most bloody and ignoble wars.

With a profound sense of the solemn and even tragical character of the step I am taking and of the grave responsibilities which it involves, but in unhesitating obedience to what I deem my constitutional duty, I advise that the Congress declare the recent course of the Imperial German Government to be in fact nothing less than war against the government and people of the United States.

The world must be made safe for democracy. Its peace must be planted upon the tested foundations of political liberty. We have no selfish ends to serve. We desire no conquest, no dominion. We seek no indemnities for ourselves, no material compensation for the sacrifices we shall freely make. We are but one of the champions of the rights of mankind. We shall be satisfied when those rights have been made as secure as the faith and the freedom of nations can make them.

Four days later, on April 6, 1917, the US Congress issued a formal declaration of war against the Imperial German Government.

Inside the White House, President Woodrow Wilson conferred with advisers and signed the proclamation of war against Germany. Everywhere there was cheering and waving of flags. Hindsight or cynicism might make us smile at the thought that this war was sometimes called That Great Adventure. Never again would we see our entry into a major conflict excite so many to such heights of elation.

All along the Western front, the Allies rejoiced. The Yanks were coming.

House, the Milner Group, the Pilgrims, the Wall Street financiers and all of those who had worked so diligently for so many years to bring Uncle Sam into war had got their wish. And before the war was over, millions more casualties would pile up.

To this day, over 100 years later, we still look back on the horrors of that "Great War" with confusion. For so long we have been told non-answers about incompetent generals and ignorant politicians. "It's the senselessness of war," the teachers of this fraudulent and partial history have told us with a shrug.

But, now that the players who worked to set the stage for this carnage have been unmasked, these questions can finally be answered.

February 21, 1916.

A week of rain, wind and heavy fog along the Western Front finally breaks, and for a moment there is silence in the hills north of Verdun. That silence is

broken at 7:15 AM when the Germans launch an artillery barrage heralding the start of the largest battle the world had ever seen.

Thousands of projectiles are flying in all directions,
some whistling, others howling, others moaning
low, and all uniting in one infernal roar. From time
to time an aerial torpedo passes, making a noise like
a gigantic motor car. With a tremendous thud a giant shell bursts quite close to our observation post,
breaking the telephone wire and interrupting all
communication with our batteries. It seems quite
impossible that he should escape in the rain of shell,
which exceeds anything imaginable; there has never
been such a bombardment in war. Our man seems
to be enveloped in explosions, and shelters himself
from time to time in the shell craters which honey-
comb the ground; finally he reaches a less stormy
spot, mends his wires, and then, as it would be madness to try to return, settles down in a big crater and
waits for the storm to pass.

When the first wave of the assault is decimated, the
ground is dotted with heaps of corpses, but the second wave is already pressing on.

This anonymous French staff officer's account of the
artillery offensive that opened the Battle of Verdun—recounting the scene as a heroic French communications officer repairs the telephone line to the
French artillery batteries, allowing for a counter-
strike against the first wave of German infantry—

137

brings a human dimension to a conflict that is beyond human comprehension. The opening salvo of that artillery barrage alone—involving 1,400 guns of all sizes—dropped a staggering 2.5 million shells on a 10-kilometre front near Verdun in northeastern France over five days of nearly uninterrupted carnage, turning an otherwise sleepy countryside into an apocalyptic nightmare of shell holes, craters, torn-out trees, and ruined villages.

By the time the battle finished 10 months later, a million casualties lay in its wake. A million stories of routine bravery, like that of the French communications officer. And Verdun was far from the only sign that the stately, sanitized version of 19th century warfare was a thing of the past. Similar carnage played out at the Somme and Gallipoli and Vimy Ridge and Galicia and a hundred other battlefields. Time and again, the generals threw their men into meat grinders, and time and again the dead bodies lay strewn on the other side of that slaughter.

But how did such bloodshed happen? For what purpose? What did the First World War *mean*?

The simplest explanation is that the mechanization of 20th century armies had changed the logic of warfare itself. In this reading of history, the horrors of World War One were the result of the logic dictated by the technology with which it was fought.

It was the logic of the siege guns that bombarded the enemy from over 100 km away. It was the logic of the poison gas, spearheaded by Bayer and their School for Chemical Warfare in Leverkusen. It was the logic of the tank, the airplane, the machine gun and all of the other mechanized implements of destruction that made mass slaughter a mundane fact of warfare.

But this is only a partial answer. More than just technology was at play in this "Great War," and military strategy and million-casualty battles were not the only ways that World War One had changed the world forever. Like that unimaginable artillery assault at Verdun, the First World War tore apart all the verities of the Old World, leaving a smoldering wasteland in its wake.

A wasteland that could be reshaped into a New World Order.

For the would-be engineers of society, war—with all of its attendant horrors—was the easiest way to demolish the old traditions and beliefs that lay between them and their goals.

This was recognized early on by Cecil Rhodes and his original clique of co-conspirators. As we have seen, it was less than one decade after the founding of Cecil Rhodes' society to achieve the "peace of the world" that that vision was amended to include war in South Africa, and then amended again to include embroiling the British Empire in a world war.

Many others became willing participants in that conspiracy because they, too, could profit from the destruction and the bloodshed.

And the easiest way to understand this idea is at its most literal level: profit.

War is a racket. It always has been.

It is possibly the oldest, easily the most profitable, surely the most vicious. It is the only one international in scope. It is the only one in which the profits are reckoned in dollars and the losses in lives.

A racket is best described, I believe, as something that is not what it seems to the majority of the people. Only a small "inside" group knows what it is about. It is conducted for the benefit of the very few, at the expense of the very many. Out of war a few people make huge fortunes.

In the World War One a mere handful garnered the profits of the conflict. At least 21,000 new millionaires and billionaires were made in the United States during that war. That many admitted their huge blood gains in their income tax returns. How many other war millionaires falsified their tax returns, no one knows.

How many of these war millionaires shouldered a rifle? How many of them dug a trench? How many of them knew what it meant to go hungry in a rat-infested dug-out? How many of them spent sleepless, frightened nights, ducking shells and shrapnel and machine gun bullets? How many of them parried a bayonet thrust of an enemy? How many of them were wounded or killed in battle?

Indeed, the war profiteering on Wall Street started even before America joined the war. Although, as J.P. Morgan partner Thomas Lamont noted, at the outbreak of the war in Europe, "American citizens were urged to remain neutral in action, in word, and even in thought, our firm had never for one moment been neutral; we didn't know how to be. From the very start we did everything we could to contribute to the cause of the Allies." Whatever the personal allegiances that may have motivated the bank's directors, this was a policy that was to yield dividends for the Morgan bank that even the greediest of bankers could scarcely have dreamed of before the war began.

John Pierpont Morgan himself died in 1913—before the passage of the Federal Reserve Act he had stewarded into existence and before the outbreak of war in Europe—but the House of Morgan stood strong, with the Morgan bank under the helm of his son, John Pierpont Morgan, Jr., maintaining its position as preeminent financier in America. The young Morgan moved quickly to leverage his family's connections with the London banking community and the Morgan bank signed its first commercial agreement with the British Army Council in January 1915, just four months into the war.

That initial contract—a $12 million purchase of horses for the British war effort to be brokered in the US by the House of Morgan—was only the beginning. By the end of the war, the Morgan bank had brokered $3 billion in transactions for the British military—equal to almost half of all-American supplies sold to the Allies in the entire war. Similar arrangements with the French, Russian, Italian, and Canadian governments saw the bank broker billions more in supplies for the Allied war effort.

But this game of war financing was not without its risks. If the Allied powers were to lose the war, the Morgan bank and the other major Wall Street banks would lose the interest on all of the credit they had extended to them. By 1917, the situation was dire. The British government's overdraft with Morgan stood at over $400 million dollars, and it was not clear that they would even win the war, let alone be in a position to repay all their debts when the fighting was over.

In April 1917, just eight days after the US declared war on Germany, Congress passed the War Loan Act, extending $1 billion in credit to the Allies. The first payment of $200 million went to the British and the entire amount was immediately handed over to Morgan as partial payment on their debt to the bank. When, a few days later, $100 million was parceled out to the French government, it, too, was promptly returned to the Morgan coffers. But the debts continued to mount, and throughout 1917 and 1918, the US Treasury—aided by the Pilgrims Society member and avowed Anglophile Benjamin Strong, president of the newly-created Federal Reserve—quietly paid off the Allied powers' war debts to J.P. Morgan.

What is interesting here is that the bankers' viewpoint. America was so deeply involved in that war financing. There was so much money which could only really be repaid as long as Britain and France won. But had they lost, the loss on the American financial stock exchange's top market—your great industrial giants—would have been horrendous. So America was deeply involved. Not the people, as is ever the case. Not the ordinary citizen who cares. But the financial establishment who had, if you like, treated the entire thing as they might a casino and put all the money on one end of the board and it had to come good for them.

The American people had no clue just how duped they were by your Carnegies, your J.P. Morgans, your great bankers, your Rockefellers, and by the other multimillionaires who emerged from that war. Because they were the ones who made the profits, not those who lost their sons, lost their grandsons, whose lives were ruined forever by war.

After America officially entered the war, the good times for the Wall Street bankers got even better.

Bernard Baruch—the powerful financier who personally led Woodrow Wilson into Democratic Party headquarters in New York "like a poodle on a string" to receive his marching orders during the 1912 election—was appointed to head the newly created "War Industries Board."

With war hysteria at its height, Baruch and the fellow Wall Street financiers and industrialists who populated the board were given unprecedented powers over manufacture and production throughout the American economy, including the ability to set quotas, fix prices, standardize products, and, as a subsequent congressional investigation showed, pad costs so that the true size of the fortunes that the war profiteers extracted from the blood of the dead soldiers was hidden from the public.

Spending government funds at an annual rate of $10 billion, the board minted many new millionaires in the American economy—millionaires who, like Samuel Prescott Bush of the infamous Bush family, happened to sit on the War Industries Board. Bernard Baruch himself was said to have personally profited from his position as head of the War Industries Board to the tune of $200 million.

The extent of government intervention in the economy would have been unthinkable just a few years before. The National War Labor Board was set up to mediate labor disputes. The Food and Fuel Control Act was passed to give the government control over the distribution and sale of food and fuel. The Army Appropriations Act of 1916 set up the Council of National Defense, populated by Baruch and other prominent financiers and industrialists, who oversaw private sector coordination with the government in transportation, industrial and farm production, financial support for the war, and public morale.

World War One was a boon for all of those who wanted to consolidate control of the many in the hands of the few. This was the vision that united all those participants in the conspiracies that led to the war itself. Beyond Cecil Rhodes and his secret society, there was a broader vision of global control for the would-be rulers of society who were seeking what tyrants had lusted after since the dawn of civilization: control of the world.

It allowed the globalists, these Anglophiles, these people who wanted the English-speaking union to reign over the whole world, militarize American thinking. Researchers found that the Carnegie Endowment for International Peace was seeking to understand how to make America a wartime economy, how to change education to get people to continually consume. It became much easier after that for the US military to advance corporate interest in Central and South America doing some horrible things to the indigenous people.

On November 11, 1918, people all over the world were celebrating, dancing in the streets, drinking champagne, hailing the Armistice that meant the end of the war. But at the front there was no celebration. Many soldiers believed the Armistice only a temporary measure and that the war would soon go on. As night came, the quietness, unearthly in its penetration, began to eat into their souls. The men sat around log fires, the first they had ever had at the front. They were trying to reassure themselves that there were no enemy batteries spying on them from the next hill and no German bombing planes approaching to blast them out of existence. They talked in low tones. They were nervous.

After the long months of intense strain, of keying themselves up to the daily mortal danger, of thinking always in terms of war and the enemy, the abrupt release from it all was physical and psychological agony. Some suffered a total nervous collapse. Some, of a steadier temperament, began to hope they would someday return to home and the embrace of loved ones. Some could think only of the crude little crosses that marked the graves of their comrades. Some fell into an exhausted sleep. All were bewildered by the sudden meaninglessness of their existence as soldiers – and through their teeming memories paraded that swiftly moving cavalcade of Cantigny, Soissons, St. Mihiel, the Meuse-Argonne and Sedan.

What was to come next? They did not know – and hardly cared. Their minds were numbed by the shock of peace. The past consumed their whole consciousness. The present did not exist-and the future was inconceivable.

World War ll was just more of the same. After engineering a war for the purpose of detaining Germany's industrial and economic progress; and making a ton of money in the process; the allied countries then exacted a heavy penalty on Germany for having defended themselves against their own destruction. Those war penalties brought Germany to its knees psychologically and economically. All this did was set the stage for a mad man to enter, and so he did. Twenty years after that human slaughter the world was about to repeat the insanity, this time with a certified mad man leading the charge.

But the war profiteers were not about to be left behind. Who financed Adolf's war efforts against the allied forces is an entirely different story, one to be told in subsequent publications

BRETTON WOODS AND
THE NEW MONETARY SYSTEM

The 1944 Bretton Woods agreement established a new global monetary system. It replaced the gold standard with the U.S. dollar as the global currency. By so doing, it established America as the dominant power in the world economy. After the agreement was signed, America was the only country with the ability to print dollars. The agreement created the World Bank and the International Monetary Fund. These U.S.-backed organizations would monitor the new system. The Bretton Woods Agreement was negotiated in July 1944 to establish a new international monetary system, the Bretton Woods System. The Agreement was developed by delegates from 44 countries at the United Nations Monetary and Financial Conference held in Bretton Woods, New Hampshire. Under the Bretton Woods System, gold was the basis for the U.S. dollar and other currencies were pegged to the U.S. dollar's value. The Bretton Woods System effectively came to an end in the early 1970s when President Richard M. Nixon announced that the U.S. would no longer exchange gold for U.S. currency. Approximately 730 delegates representing 44 countries met in Bretton Woods in July 1944 with the principal goals of creating an efficient foreign exchange system, preventing competitive devaluations of currencies, and promoting international economic growth. The Bretton Woods Agreement and System were central to these goals. The Bretton Woods Agreement also created two important organizations—the International Monetary Fund (IMF) and the World Bank. While the Bretton Woods System was dissolved in the 1970s, both the IMF and World

Bank have remained strong pillars for the exchange of international currencies. Though the Bretton Woods conference itself took place over just three weeks, the preparations for it had been going on for several years. The primary designers of the Bretton Woods System were the famous British economist John Maynard Keynes and American Chief International Economist of the U.S. Treasury Department Harry Dexter White. Keynes' hope was to establish a powerful global central bank to be called the Clearing Union and issue a new international reserve currency called the Bancorp. White's plan envisioned a more modest lending fund and a greater role for the U.S. dollar, rather than the creation of a new currency. In the end, the adopted plan took ideas from both, leaning more toward White's plan. It wasn't until 1958 that the Bretton Woods System became fully functional. Once implemented, its provisions called for the U.S. dollar to be pegged to the value of gold. Moreover, all other currencies in the system were then pegged to the U.S. dollar's value. The exchange rate applied at the time set the price of gold at $35 an ounce.

At that time, every single dollar bill was backed by and was exchangeable for gold. That kept all currencies very stable in relationship to each other. The prices were fixed, the fluctuations were minor and individuals the world over could start businesses confident that their money was always going to be of value.

IN 1971 as a result of the falling US dollar, prompted by the international capital flow into gold, and the funding of the Vietnam War, President Richard opted to take the US dollar off the gold standard. It left the dollar floating, back by nothing, and this is how it has been since 1971. Inescapably, all other currencies that were backed by the US dollar were also worth nothing tangible only trust in the American government. Money backed by nothing is known as fiat currency, which in Latin means, *let it be done*. In other words, it is money, so it is. It's value rest entirely in the full faith and trust of the people that use it. But how can the people of Latin America and the rest of the world be expected to have full faith and trust in the United States currency?

The consequences of having money backed by nothing is that whenever the Federal reserve creates money out of thin air as it is their only way to do it, it dilutes the currency supply of all other nations that depends on the US dollar, all country's reserve are worth less each time money is created. In the past few decades the United States has been printing and producing trillions of dollars with the confidence that the world will just accept it even though it is backed by nothing. Fiat, or faith, is born out of the fact that nobody knows where money comes from.

A central bank is essentially the entity that manages the nation's money supply, and it can lend money to the government with interest. And so it does to the average citizen who wishes to purchase a home or a car. When they take out a loan, it is recorded by the bank as an asset. Debt then becomes money. In the words of Mariner Eccles, former governor of the Federal Reserve: "If there were no debts in the money system, there wouldn't be any money." So instead of gold being the backing of the US, it is now debt. So countries and people must now be more and deeper in debt in order for the system to stay afloat. If people and governments stop taking out loans, and pay back the debt they owe, the debt doesn't grow, the money supply shrinks and the system collapses.

As bizarre as it sounds, that is the reality of our economic system. It and other central banks around the world control money by adjusting its supply and the cost of borrowing it by way of interest rates. With these tools and as a consequence of what is referred to as crowd psychology Central Banks control booms and busts in the economy at will. They can also stall and derail an economy simply by messing with it. A good example is the 2008 housing collapse.

At a congressional hearing on August 12, 2004 the then chairman of the Federal Reserve Board Alan Greenspan stated in response to a questioning by Paul Ryan on the subject of private social security account: *There is nothing to stop the federal government from printing as much money as it wants and giving it to whoever it wants.*

In 2000, Alan Greenspan lowered the interest rate to 1% in order to fight off a recession from the dot com bubble collapse encouraging people to borrow money. Greenspan thought that he could create a wealth effect that people would start to buy houses, that the value of these homes would go up and as a result people would feel wealthier and spend more money in the economy thereby stimulating it. The plan worked for a while, but the people borrowed too much and the result of this was a housing bubble. This constitutes a prime example of what could go wrong when central banks mess with the economy. No doubt, the corrupt bankers have a lot to answer for in their role in the crisis the feds have a far bigger long-term effect.

THE CURRENT CRISIS

It may be argued that all historic periods are complex, and that the one we experience today is no different in its level of complexity. People are confused and at a lost for meaning in their lives.

At the core of the problem is the fact that the species; almost in its entirety; continues to allow itself to be tripped up by mythology and childish thinking, even after the extraordinary scientific revelations of the past two hundred years.

It goes without saying that a childish mind cannot solve complex problems. A simple example of this childish thinking is the vast number of humans denouncing science while clutching their cellular telephone, one of the greatest achievements in science of all times. There have been other significant achievements in science in our times but none hold sway over us as a specie as the cellular telephone has.

The front cover depiction of planet earth approximately 2 billion years ago in the book that accompanies this publication, is at the core of all of the manifestations made in these pages, and as painful as it is the separation is between those who can conceptualize this reality, and those who refuse to, or are unable to embrace this complex reality is where we begin.

The embracing of this reality puts aside all notions of God or Jesus or Mohammed or Allah, or Buda, or the gazillion other deities invented by humans, together with the dangerous belief systems built around them.

At the International Center for intellectual Development all of our books and articles are done in English and Spanish, this is because these are the two languages in which its leaders are educated in and where they have most of their following.

Speaking of Latin America in particular, the manifestations against manipulation in this area has been loud and clear. People are beginning to understand the level of cruelty and filth that resides in the minds of those that refer to themselves as politicians.

The most disconcerting aspect of the liberation movement in Latin America is that as they attempt to function as revolutionaries, forging drastic changes in their respective countries, they too embrace the silly notions of the people that currently oppress them, the notion that 2000 years ago a man walked on water, or that a human being rose up to heaven after his death. It is even insidious that the only people that rise to heaven are men. This level of confusion produces nothing good. The debates and discussions on the subject simply go around in circles because these are undeveloped minds attempting to deal with the manipulation coming from people who are far cleverer that they are. A sad few are aware of the mechanisms of manipulation that were erected in the past century to keep them poor and confused. They make reference to the neoliberal model of governing that is aimed at keeping a few people rotten rich and the rest of the population impoverished. Put simply, the dots are not being connected.

NEOLIBERALISM

The oppressed people of the world have so far identified ne-oliberalism as the source of their present conflict, but few really understand the meaning of the term.

The issue is confusing for those of us who identify ourselves as liberals since this has always had a positive connotation. Not only that we all had to work our way through liberal studies courses in college in order to advance to more difficult courses, so the term came as a shock to us when it appeared as if liberalism was now classified as a bad thing.

The term was taken from the French word *Laisses faire,* and that term itself originated in a meeting that took place around 1681 between powerful French Controller-General of Finances Jean-Baptiste Colbert and a group of French businessmen headed by M. Le Gendre. When the eager bureaucrat asked how the French state could be of service to the merchants and help pro-mote their commerce, Le Gendre replied simply: "Laissez-nous faire" ("Leave it to us" or "Let us do [it]"

The confusion with the term arose from the Spanish interpre-tation of the expression. In Spanish Laisses faire was interpreted as Liberalismo, as it was seen as business men and women asking to be left alone as they attempt to conduct their businesses. It re-fers to an abstention of the government from interfering in the business sector or what has come to be known as the free market. In Spanish the term is defined as *Liberalismo Económico.* These ideas described economic liberalization policies such as privati-zation, austerity, deregulation, free trade and reductions in government spending in order to increase the role of the private sector in the economy and society These market-based ideas and the policies they inspired constitute a paradigm shift away from the approach of the British economist John Maynard Keynes, after the second world war. Keynesian economics is a theory that says the government should increase demand to boost growth. Keynesians believe consumer demand is the primary driving force in an economy. As a result, the theory supports expansionary fiscal policy. Its main tools are government spending on infrastructure, unemployment benefits, and education.

Obviously, economic liberalism never worked in France as the French have always had security measures in place for workers while also making sure that merchants did not take advantage of the public to whom they sold their goods.

The term went out of favor for more than 2 centuries and was reintroduced in Chile by the government of Augusto Pinochet as a new form of Liberalism or Neo-liberalism. Chile thus became the poster child for this new version of a rather criminal approach to government in which social services are slashed and the corporate class is allowed to do as it pleased with the populace.

In addition, the central tenet of neoliberalism is the privatization of all governmental services that could be deemed profitable. This is based on the notion that the private sector is more efficient at managing the services needed by the public.

The attempt to introduce those archaic, antihuman policies became known as Neo-liberalism, a new form of liberalism. The term entered into common use in the 1980s in connection with Augusto Pinochet's economic reforms in Chile, and it quickly became a term with negative connotations.

Pinochet's market-oriented reform policies such as "eliminating price controls, deregulating capital markets, lowering trade barriers" and reducing state influence in the economy, especially through privatization and austerity worked well for a small minority in Chile, but life among the poor and middle class became unbearable.

Subsequent administrations in Chile have taken steps to modify the laws regarding the free market economic policies in the country but this has not been easy. To make matters worse, when the right-wing leaning government of Sebastian Pineda attempted to raise prices on the Subway fares the people has had enough. The movement was led by young people who decided to jump the turnstiles rather than going along with the governments continued repressive measures.

THE LATIN-AMERICAN REALITY

Those of us born in Latin America or that follow the development in that area have undergone an emotional roller coaster with the ups and downs of the alternating political groups that seem to take charge in the Latin-American nations in a relatively short period.

The roller coaster involves the hope that was experienced at the turn of the century when Hugo Chavez, a military officer, risked death in order to rescue his country's oil wealth to purchase luxury apartments and homes in Miami and Europe. This of course was after their American oil partners had walked off with the lion share of the oil profits. The country however, had remain impoverished.

It had remained a rather peaceful country despite decades of military rule. This was unusual. Latin America had experienced military rule in Argentina and Chile in particular, where tens of thousands of young people had been systematically murdered for opposing the country's oppressive regimes. As unusual as this may sound Venezuela always had a humane military. Chavez failed in his first intent to take power and he was not killed, instead they took him out of their jails and begged him to take over the country, recognizing that they had failed miserably. For that and other reasons Venezuela is the heart of progressive Latin Americans, and at the center of all Latin American issues. The country's oil reserve was discovered in 1922 and it turned out to be twice as large as that of Saudi Arabia. But in addition to oil the country is awashed in precious minerals. It has the largest deposit of Gold, Thorium, and Coltan, the latter being often referred to as Blue Gold. Coltan represents the key ingredient in cellular telephones and satellite internal memory processing.

One has to keep in mind that of the 8 billion people on the planet nearly everyone owns a cellular telephone.

The wealth these minerals represent is enormous, it is enough for Venezuela, together with Mexico, the second wealthiest country in Latin America and the Caribbean, to be declared the Capital of that region.

Few thinking Latin Americans would object to such grand and far reaching proposals. The fact is that these two countries are fortunate enough to possess the natural wealth that allow them and the rest of Latin America to stand up to the brutality of the American and Western European forces. All that is needed is a concerted effort on the part of all of Latin America to identify and stamp out the kind of corruption that has prevented this region from growing as it should in areas of the intellect, finance, education, health and industry.

That much natural wealth under the control of dark skinned people is frightening to the United States government, particularly under Republican regimes. What is more, in all of his speeches Nicolas Maduro refers to himself as Black, as did Hugo Chavez when he was alive. The Bolivarian government went overboard in making sure the wealth of the country was spread among its people. Critics will argue that to some extent they may have extended themselves, but it was for the people's benefit. Chavez was a military coronel who got tired of supporting the Oligarchs' plunder of the country's wealth so he placed his own life on the line in an attempt to save the country from the vultures bent on destroying it. His most ardent supporter was Maduro, so he made him Vice President. But Maduro is the first to admit he was a mere bus driver when Chavez chose him, and he vowed that if he was to lose the popular elections he would step away from power as the constitution commands him to do. The problem in this case is that the opposition is deeply divided, and the young man who proclaimed himself president has never earned more than 90.000 votes and that is for a small district he represented. Guaido is widely known as a vulgar violent paramilitary responsible for burning upwards of 30 Black government supporters alive. His recent sabotage of the electricity grid caused the death of 17 patients who were on life support machines. These murders are laid to the feet of the young man who has the support of Mike Pence and vast numbers of Christians. A photo of Guaido baring his ass to the cameras is currently circulating on the web. It offers a clearer picture of the insane vulgarity and low quality of the supposed president.

For a background on the current made up crisis, one can cite Glen Greenwald's statement that *Every major US war of the past few decades began the same way; that is, The government fabricates an inflammatory and emotionally provocative lie which large media outlets uncritically treats as truth. Meanwhile they would refuse to listen to or air the dissenting voices thus inflaming primal anger against the country the United States government wishes to attack.*

While Donald Trump, Mike Pence and Marco Rubio eagerly plan a wholesale slaughter of the Venezuelan civilians, contemporaneous videos are circling with Venezuelans going about their normal daily routine. Often times these videos are shot on some of the massive new residential developments the Bolivarian government created for its people.

As it relates to Mexico, it is interesting to note that despite its monetary crisis in the recent past and a major flue pandemic and massive migration of their citizens to the United States, there was never an attempt to invade Mexico. Of course, the answer to that may very well be that Mexico never attempted to establish a socialist government although a good number of the social policies amount to precisely that.

Among the countries with a history of having faced the kind of economic crisis Venezuela is currently experiencing are: Argentina, Mexico, Zimbabwe, Germany and the United States. Given its natural wealth there is no question that Venezuela will ride this wake and emerge victorious at the end of this process with it benevolent and productive social system intact. What Venezuela must have at the moment is the support of all persons of good will particularly those in Latin America and the Caribbean. Its experimental model sets a new pace for the emerging egalitarianism that must take place globally.

The efforts on the part of the United States government to prevent Mexico from industrializing was made clear in a Dec. 26-Jan. 8, 1979 Executive Intelligence Review called U.S Report 43. The U.S. policy emerged in portions of a classified policy review document, called Presidential Review Memorandum 41 (PRM-41), leaked to the Washington Post Dec. 15 by Brzezinski's office at the National Security Council. As predicted two months ago in this journal (Vol. V,No. 42, Oct. 31), and now confirmed with a vengeance, PRM-41 outlines a series of "options" to Carter for "improved U.S.-Mexico relations." Its every feature implies strangulation of Mexican industry and development, and brutal pressure tactics to gain control of Mexico's enormous oil and gas reserves.

Progressive Latin Americans, including Afro Latinos, have been elated over the fact that the people of Mexico have finally insisted that their choice of a progressive government be respected. For decades the progressives of have accused the established parties of robbing them of the election and plundering the country's coffers. Andres Manuel Lopez Obrador has become a breath of fresh air for those of us who sat on pins and needles over the course the region would be taking. In addition, shortly after AMLO was elected, the people of Argentina throughout their own neoliberal government, and the other two neoliberal governments in Ecuador, Chile and Peru are faced with stiff opposition from the overwhelming majority of their population.

THE AWAKENING

Four hundred years ago research conducted by the Polish scientist Nicolas Copernicus revealed to the world that the Sun does not revolve around our planet. Those findings were suppressed however, as the powerful religious institutions of his time would have executed for going against the sacred edicts of the church. Much more has been revealed since then but unfortunately these extraordinary scientific revelations have not made their way into the subconscious of the overwhelming majority of humans. That precisely is the reasoning behind this new proposal. The term Scientific Psychology is thus introduced to describe the relationship that should exist between the scientific discoveries in all of the ages, and the practice of psychology, or more specifically, psychotherapy. My own experience in more than three decades of psychotherapy says that the introduction of this factual evidentiary information has the potential of inoculating the individual against delusion and against the massive confusion that forever engulfs the masses.

Since time immemorial, scientific researchers have been bringing us information about ourselves and the world in which we live, and the cosmological scenery that is presented with this information.

This information of course, is far removed from nearly everything humans have been told by the clergy of various stripes and denominations. The self-discovery it offers holds promise for the future as the stranglehold that religion continues to have on the mind of the masses is lessened. The ignorance, the prejudice, and

162

the racism that is supported by narrow religious teachings will also decrease as these findings make it into the subconscious.

Thanks to scientists the psychological playing field has been leveled, despite the fact that the information has not gotten to all quarters. It is therefore only a matter of time as precise information about our common stock and our common origins as a species take hold with new generations of humans on this planet.

The Center for Intellectual Development, a not for profit organization legally registered in the State of Florida and in Costa Rica, has had great success in the use of scientific psychology both in its therapeutic interventions and in its educational seminars. It is empowering because it removes the notion of victim that most survivors of abuse carry, and it prepares them to take charge of their own lives as they assert themselves in a world that is distinctively theirs.

It is not rocket science, in fact the method is alarmingly simple. The only difficulty facing this new method is the hypnotic and narcotizing effect the various religious forms has had on the overwhelming majority of the population. For those who are no longer under the spell of religion this method has far reaching effects.

My partiality towards the intellect is one I could not shake even if I wanted to, for I've read and witnessed too much unnecessary sufferings purely on account of its absence. I may succeed at persuading only a few to the cause of intellectual development, but those few are a cause for great celebration given the reality of our times. I will be bringing this organization to anyone open enough to listen, and in so doing branches will be developed in any corner of the world where people are willing to relate to each other with open-mindedness, with love, and with compassion.

As stated, much has happened since that first attempt where, my eternal optimism leads me to focus on the subject of human happiness. I was concerned about the pain and confusion in which so many people live their lives, but half way through it I realized that a lot of this suffering is self-inflicted not realizing fully that the one thing that is needed to overcome a state of poverty and misery is information. However, for reasons that I find difficult to explain, people in general prefer to remain uninformed about the most vital issues concerning their lives. They prefer to remain infantile, believing that there is a father figure somewhere beyond the skies who sooner or later will make everything right. They refuse to become involved in the hard work that is involved in acquiring information, and they are afraid that being informed will inevitably force them to act. So being uninformed makes everything easier. Whatever the reason, people in general chose to remain ignorant. It has become their comfort zone, and despite their complaining, they're happy in that zone. This constituted the ultimate education for me but I couldn't turn back, I was already committed, so I was forced to alter my course of action. This could no longer be a book about happiness but rather, one that identifies and deals with the cause of misery. True to self I had to point out ignorance and stupidity as the primary cause of most human suffering. This will no doubt irate a great many, but there is simply no other way of putting it. In an era so replete with information one has to make an effort to remain ignorant, regrettably most people are making that effort. I'm not suggesting that knowledge alone will cure all human suffering, for given the work that I do I'm aware that there are those who are genuinely ill, struggling to overcome the traumas inflicted on them when they were only babies of four, and seven and 10 years old, some even older. My heart goes out to those, and it is for them that this book is written. My associates and I are determined to create a place where these suffering individuals; most of whom are extremely talented; can find solace, can find peace comfort and strength. It is not for the Smart Alex' who have all the answers; in fact, it is not even recommended that they read this book for it would do them no good. The ***Center for Intellectual Development*** has created a place for all those who wish to free themselves from their own suffering. That is our only goal. But one cannot be a part of this process while holding on to the very things that has made their lives miserable, something must give. In this process everything we've ever held sacred is up for scrutiny, and if it doesn't pass the test it will be abolished. Culture and belief systems are at the core of everyone's existence, yet few of us know what they are. If we had to give a simple and short definition for what we've come to regard as Culture, it would be ***learned behavior***. Belief, unfortunately, is something we are forced to do before we even learn how to think. Wherever belief supersedes thinking that society is doomed. One only has to look at the socio-economic state of Black People today to realize what happens when a people place belief above thinking. They were given a set of beliefs by their slave masters, and they continue to clutch these long after the master had set them free. They fail to realize that they were only set free because the master no longer had use for them, he had developed machinery that could do the work faster and more efficiently. Their efforts had

165

little or nothing to do with the master's decision to set them free although he has allowed them to think that it was their struggle for liberation that made it happen. I suppose some dignity was preserved by allowing them to think that, but the delusion it encouraged also caused permanent damage in the psyche of these ex-slaves for it almost forced them to see the master as benevolent and full of compassion. This delusion of course, causes them to be eternally grateful to their former masters, and nothing could be more damaging.

I have great respect for those who dedicate themselves to this lonely and often unrewarding profession. I became involved in this business of writing only because no one else is willing to say the things that I find to be compelling. I've learned a great deal in the process but I would just as soon have someone else do the writing while I dedicate time to my real passions that are: building, cooking, mentoring and organizing. I organize because of the love I have for my fellow humans, and this undying love has made a scholar out of me and the driving force behind my desire to learn all that I can about self and others. It is why I have ventured into the field of history, psychology and philosophy. The ultimate objective of the organization is the emotional and economic stability of all its members. All children are considered honorary members of this organization regardless of their parent's mindset. We will forever fight for their rights to be treated with love, kindness and respect regardless of their behavior.

We've decided in this organization that there is only one enemy to be fought against, and that is *ignorance*, none other, and as far as we are concerned the only weapons needed in this battle are: ***Wisdom, Knowledge, and Greater Understanding.***

ALICE MILLER (1923-2010)

We learn from Miller (1984) that this giant of the field of psychology was born to a Jewish family in Poland and was trained as a psychoanalysis in Switzerland obtaining her doctorate in 1953.

In 1980, after having worked as a psychoanalyst and an analyst trainer for 20 years, Miller suspended her practice and dedicated herself to exploring the issue of childhood. She was critical of both Sigmund Freud and Carl Jung for ignoring this issue and several others in their practice and in their writings. Her first three books originated from research she took upon herself as a response to what she felt were major blind spots in her field. However, by the time her fourth book was published, she no longer believed that psychoanalysis was viable in any respect. In 1985 Miller wrote about the research from her time as a psychoanalyst: "For twenty years I observed people denying their childhood traumas, idealizing their parents and resisting the truth about their childhood by any means."

According to Miller (2002), despite all of Stalin's power, he spent his lifetime in fear of his father. Regarding Hitler, she stated he believed that the annihilation of millions of people would free him of the tormenting fear of his violent alcoholic father. *Poisonous Pedagogy,* in her opinion, contributed a great deal in millions of children and adults supporting Hitler's atrocities without experiencing a sense of horror. Hitler and his cohorts, she argued, were part of a generation of children who had been exposed to brutal physical correction and humiliation, and who later vented their pent-up feeling of anger and helpless rage on innocent victims. Safe in the knowledge that they were doing so with the Fuhrer's blessings, they were finally able to give free reign to those feelings without fear of punishment. Her claim is that wherever cruelty and humiliation are a part of parenting, those methods will be reflected in the behavior of young people.

Miller (2010), further states that in the name of good parenting millions of children all over the world are subjected to some of the worst form of violence. Mao Tse Tung was the son a strict teacher who set out to drum obedience and wisdom into him with the aid of severe physical correction. Mao later attempted to install this same philosophy in his country at the cost of more than thirty-five million lives. Like *Hitler, Joseph Stalin* was exposed to incredible brutality as a child. Stalin's brutal treatment at the hands of an alcoholic father made his childhood pain with dread of being killed during one of his father's outbursts. As an adult, he had the power to fend off that fear by humiliating others.

In short what we learn from Miller (2010) and nearly all of her publications and interviews is that worldwide violence has its roots in the fact that children are beaten all over the world, especially during their first years of life, when their brains become structured. She said that the damage caused by this practice is devastating, but this subject is hardly discussed in our society. She adds that the suppression of their natural reactions like rage and fear generated by their inability to defend themselves against the violence inflicted on them forces them to discharge these strong emotions later as adults against their own children or whole nations. The example she often points to is Adolf Hitler whose childhood was filled with violence coming from an alcoholic father. Violence towards the child in the form of beating and humiliating not only produces unhappy and confused children, but also confused, irrational adults who in turn create dysfunctional and irrational societies. Miller concludes that only when our societies become aware of these complex dynamics will we break this insidious chain of violence.

The concept of Moral Injury may be worth looking into, particularly since it has everything to do with notorious acts of violence that are perpetrated against large numbers of human beings. Exploring whether some sense of guilt or remorse is experienced by the perpetrator is the psychological phenomenon that this term was originally intended to deal with.

Vargas (2013) defined Moral Injury as that complex feeling that arises in the individual after perpetrating, failing to prevent, or bearing witness to acts that is beyond that individuals deeply held moral beliefs and expectations. The literature on two of the world's worst mass murderers reveal that they were deeply religious, or at least were brought up in religious households. The question that is asked is whether the element of Moral Injury played a role at any point in these men's life since according to the literature Moral injury can lead to serious distress, depression and suicidality. In April 1987 Miller announced in an interview with the German magazine *Psychologie Heute* (Psychology Today) her rejection of psychoanalysis. The following year she cancelled her memberships in both the Swiss Psychoanalytic Society and the International Psychoanalytic Association, because she felt that psychoanalytic theory and practice made it impossible for former victims of child abuse to recognize the violations inflicted on them and to resolve the consequences of the abuse,[10] as they "remained in the old tradition of blaming the child and protecting the parents.

Miller blamed psychologically abusive parents for the majority of neurosis and psychosis. She maintained that all instances of mental illness, addiction, crime and cultism were ultimately caused by suppressed rage and pain as a result of subconscious childhood trauma that was not resolved emotionally, assisted by a helper, which she came to term an "enlightened witness." In all cultures, "sparing the parents is our supreme law," wrote Miller. Even psychiatrists, psychoanalysts and clinical psychologists were unconsciously afraid to blame parents for the mental disorders of their clients, she contended. According to Miller, mental health professionals were also creatures of the poisonous pedagogy internalized in their own childhood. This explained why the command "Honor thy parents" was one of the main targets in Miller's school of psychology.

Miller called electroconvulsive therapy "a campaign against the act of remembering." In her book, *Abbruch der Schweigemauer* (The Demolition of Silence), she criticized psychotherapists' advice to clients to forgive their abusive parents, arguing that this could only hinder recovery through remembering and feeling childhood pain. It was her contention that the majority of therapists fear this truth and that they work under the influence of interpretations culled from both Western and Oriental religions, which preach forgiveness by the once-mistreated child. She believed that forgiveness did not resolve hatred, but covered it in a dangerous way in the grown adult: displacement on scapegoats, as she discussed in her psycho-biographies of Adolf Hitler and Jürgen Bartsch, both of whom she described as having suffered severe parental abuse. A common denominator in Miller's writings is her explanation of why human beings prefer not to know about their own victimization during childhood: to avoid unbearable pain. She believed that the unconscious command of the individual, not to be aware of how he or she was treated in childhood, led to displacement: the irresistible drive to repeat abusive parenting in the next generation of children or direct unconsciously the unresolved trauma against others (war, terrorism, delinquency) or against him or herself (eating disorders, drug addiction, depression).

Miller (2010) states that worldwide violence has its roots in the fact that children are beaten all over the world, especially during their first years of life, when their brains become structured. She said that the damage caused by this practice is devastating, but unfortunately hardly noticed by society. She argued that as children are forbidden to defend themselves against the violence inflicted on them, they must suppress the natural reactions like rage and fear, and they discharge these strong emotions later as adults against their own children or whole peoples: "child abuse like beating and humiliating not only produces unhappy and confused children, not only destructive teenagers and abusive parents, but thus also a confused, irrationally functioning society. Miller stated that only through becoming aware of this dynamic can we break the chain of violence.

For an example of the calamity we as a species expose ourselves to when we ill-treat children and deny them the healing they deserve we need to go no further than Adolf Hitler. Waite

171

(1971) presented a highly researched and carefully thought-out paper on Hitler. In it he explains that six million Jews were sacrificed to Hitler's personal sense of unworthiness and hyper vulnerability of the body to filth and decay. So great were Hitler's anxieties about these things, so crippled was he psychically, that he seems to have had to develop a unique perversion to deal with them, to triumph over them. He added that: "Hitler gained sexual satisfaction by having a young woman squat over him to urinate or defecate on his head." This was his "private religion": his personal transcendence of his anxiety, the hyper experience and resolution of it. This was a personal trip that he laid not only on the Jews and the German nation but directly on his mistresses. It is highly significant that each of them committed suicide or tried to do so and more than a simple coincidence. It might very possibly be that they could not stand the burden of his perversion; the whole of it was on them, it was theirs to live with — not in itself, as a simple and disgusting physical act, but in its shattering absurdity and massive incongruity with the role he was playing at the time. The man who is the object of all social worship, the hope of Germany and the world, the victor over evil and filth, is the same one who will in an hour plead with you in private to "be nice" to him with the fullness of your excretions. I would say that this discordance between private and public esthetics is possibly too much to bear, unless one can get some kind of commanding height or vantage point from which to mock it or otherwise dismiss it, say, as a prostitute would by considering her client a simple pervert, an inferior form of life. (p. 234). Lloyd deMause, a collaborator and close friend of Alice Miller has arrived at similar conclusions. He stated in deMause (1974):

172

The history of childhood is a nightmare from which contemporary society has only recently began to awaken. The further back in history one goes, the lower the level of child care, and the more likely children are to be killed, abandoned, beaten, terrorized, and sexually abused. (p. 1)

deMause's continuous reference to psychogenics reminds readers of the possible relationship that may exist between current socio-economic problems and the treatment meted out to children for nearly all human history as each traumatized generation of children acts out their repressed resentment and anger as adults. He argues that the central force for change in society is neither technology nor economics, but the psychogenic changes in personality occurring because of successive generations of parent child interactions. Therefore, examine how children were valued and conceptualized over time can help to better understand the emergence and evolution of violence directed at children.

CELEBRATING HUMANITY

Notwithstanding the massive confusion that now engulfs the lives of nearly all members of the species; some time can be taken out to celebrate all that the specie has accomplished. We celebrate the science that gave us our much beloved cellular telephone, and cannot imagine our lives without it.

Those of us who have already achieved this level of thinking have decided against participating in any of the childish debates regarding god, belief or religion, and to relate to our fellow human beings solely on the bases of what we already agree on to possess in common. Some of the things we would hope to have in common are:

1- Creating a much better world for future generations, one that is based on reason, fairness and justice.

2- Empowering fair-minded people of all backgrounds to assert themselves despite the usual threats and intimidations people of good will invariably face when they manifest themselves.

3- Protecting healthiness of the environment 8 billion members of the species depend on for life and reproduction.

The Center for Intellectual Development, in association with Club Vizcaya International sponsors a series of concerts that celebrates humanity as it is, with all of its faults and its confusions. We've overcome Infanticide we've overcome widespread state sponsored slavery, we've overcome state condone rape and abuse of all type. This alone is a lot to celebrate, and that is the reason for our concerts and the people involved in promoting them.

The above examples are evidence that a better world has already been created, and it testifies to the fact that much more work is left to be done as we move to create a better world, one that is filled with meaningful dialogue fairness and justice.

We purposely leave out the term tolerance because it has been used a great deal as it relates to people with sexual natures other than that of heterosexual. The term is reserved to people of the LGBTQ communities, where the larger society has abrogated the right to tolerate these fellow humans. In celebrating humanity, the sacred rights of every human being to live happily is what we promote, and will battle anyone who aim at restricting those rights from any of our fellow humans because of the nature of their attraction.

Out of pure ignorance and religious nonsense, members of this community were made to suffer for centuries, especially after religions were invented. We now understand the complex nature of sexuality and sexual attraction, and we are immensely humbler as a result of this understanding.

Our concerts raise the funds needed for promoting a new system of building that create contemporary homes that are earthquake, fire and hurricane resistant, with accessible flat roof. At the moment getting this program off the ground constitute the greatest of all challenges, but it must be done.

If the overwhelming majority of the human race continues to toil in the darkest of ignorance, that is, ignorance as it relates to some of the most vital information about themselves ie; their own beginnings, their own humble origins, only one group can be blamed for it. That group undoubtedly is the academic class. It is important that we start from the top of that class which what has come to be known as the Ivy League Institutions. As research institutions these schools set the standards for what should be taught at all academic centers in the country and around the world. The tragedy of this is that these institutions, despite their stature and the glory given to them by the public at large, are in essence *Religious Institutions* lending support and endorsement to the childishness that is at the foundation of the *Abrahamic Faiths*. This religious trilogy created by what we define as the Abrahamic Faiths (Judaism, Christianity and Islam) is responsible for a great deal of human suffering. This is not to say that other invented religions like Buddhism, Hinduism, and Zoroastrianism among countless others, have not done their share of damage, the reality is that these three are the most influential in the times we live in. For all of their fame and glory, these Ivy League institutions are no more than giant churches masquerading as intellectual centers. The irony of this reality was underscored when the only African American president, a graduate of one of these institutions, declared his allegiance to Jesus Christ a mythical character not unlike that of Abraham or Moses. No one is sure who created Moses or how he was created, what we do know however is that Abraham before him was a figment of Moses' imagination. Not only that, the inventor of the Moses character makes him the writer of the *Pentateuch,* the first 5 books of the bible. In these 5 books the character of Abraham was created, and he was given powers that no other human had had up until that time, the power to see and speak to the god they'd recently invented. Approximately two thousand years later Jew residing in Greece, known as Hellenistic Jews, came up with the character of Jesus. With skillful manipulation the story took on a life of its own. The rest is history, and you challenge it at the risk of your own life, just as I am doing with these writings.

If all of the focus is on the evidence, it is infantile to spend time discussing mythology. Mythology is satisfying to some as they curl up into that world of imagination and comfort. But it does not work for science or the scientific mind. The scientific mind must have not just the facts but the actual evidence behind that so-called fact. At a time when we can work our way back to the birth of the Universe 14 billion years ago, who has the time to study the life, real or not, of men and women who lived and died just 2 or 3 thousand years ago.

Being human is all that matters today, and to be human is to embrace the totality of the experience of the modern members of this species which is only approximately 100.000 years old.

Born in Africa this species is still struggling to know itself, and the horrendous history of Africa does not make it any better. Everyone came out of Africa, waves of migration out of the continent produced multiple skin tones and physical characteristics, characteristics we've come to refer to as races. These races; another human invention not unlike religion and so many other concepts that have no bases in reality; are the source of much human suffering. Africa as the cradle of humankind and the birthplace of civilization is a foregone conclusion, at the highest academic circles this is no longer a debate. What is sad and pathetic is that they have not ventured to explain this to the ignorant masses. Perhaps it is because the masses are dugged so deep into their ignorance that words of wisdom on the part of the scientist would not get through. The time per hour is worth too much to be spent on the backward elements who without any factual information whatsoever convince themselves they're in the position to converse with, or worse yet, debate with scientists. Unfortunately, such is the case with the masses, few are willing to listen, and fewer yet are open-minded enough to allow evidentiary knowledge to take hold.

The fear of death is a uniquely human sentiment, one that came only with self-awareness. But scientists have been in a unique position to convince us that *life is energy, and energy never dies*. This is a simple and comforting response to our generalized fear of death

OUR EARTH'S PROTECTIVE LAYERS

The formation of the five invisible layers that protect the earth from the sun's ultraviolet rays and other threatening objects is another miracle we are yet to understand. Those five layers are:

1-The **troposphere** is the layer closest to Earth's surface. It is 4 to 12 miles thick and contains half of Earth's atmosphere.

2-The **stratosphere** is the second layer. It starts above the troposphere and ends about 31 miles (50 km) above ground. Ozone is abundant here and it heats the atmosphere while also absorbing harmful radiation from the sun. The air here is very dry, and it is about a thousand times thinner here than it is at sea level. It is the layer in which jet aircraft and weather balloons operate.

3- The **mesosphere** starts at 31 miles (50 km) and extends to 53 miles (85 km) high. The top of the mesosphere, called the mesopause, is the coldest part of Earth's atmosphere with temperatures averaging about minus 130 degrees F (minus 90 C). This layer is hard to study. Jets and balloons don't go high enough to study, and the orbit of satellites and space shuttles is just too high for them to take samples of that air. This is also where meteors burn up on their way to impact the earth.

4-The **thermosphere** extends from about 56 miles (90 km) to between 310 and 620 miles (500 and 1,000 km). Temperatures can get up to minus 2,700 degrees F (1,500 C) at this altitude. The thermosphere is considered part of Earth's atmosphere, but air density is so low that most of this layer is what is normally thought of as outer space. In fact, this is where the space shuttle flew in its time, and where the International Space Station is located at the moment. The aurora borealis and the aurora australis take place in this atmospheric layer. In this colorful phenomenon charged particles from space collide with atoms and molecules in the thermosphere, converting them into higher states of energy. The atoms shed this excess energy by emitting photons of light that produce the spectacle.

5-The **exosphere**, the highest layer, is extremely thin and is where the atmosphere merges into outer space. It is composed of very widely dispersed particles of hydrogen and helium.

COMMENTARY

The preceding is by far the most plausible explanation we have for the birth of this planet and the multiplicity of life form on its surface. It is not intended to be a lesson in astroscience but rather a presentation of some of the most basic information members are expected to manage in order to function effectively within the ranks of the Center for Intellectual Development. Our therapeutic interventions begin with this basic information, and it is designed not only to remove the notion of victimhood in our clients but also to empower them with a dose of the actual reality that brought about their existence.

This information levels the playing field as far as human relation is concerned. Where religion or religious belief sits within all of this is anyone's guess but it is not a part of our conversation. All thinking and all analysis must include this ultimate reality, without it the exercise is futile.

Today most treatment centers make reference to reality base therapy and brag about their ability to implement their version of this new approach. It is one of the few cases in which reality is accepted as a relative concept. It is almost as if they are redefining the term reality since in many cases these treatment centers subscribe to ideas principles and belief systems that are the furthest from reality. They treat patients with delusion and distorted thought processes while they themselves embrace the idea that a man is responsible for the creation of the world we know and everything in it. This delusional thinking has defined human affairs since time immemorial.

THE POWER OF KNOWLEDGE

Ten years ago, I published a book entitled The Human Experience. It was before I entered graduate school thus my writing skills and my patience as a scholar were not yet formulated. The re-publication of that book is still in the works but I've extracted this section for this booklet because of its relevance. The purpose of this is to keep our overall reality always in focus and above everything else. It reminds constantly that everything we do and everything that happens to us; regardless of its horror or intensity; is still a part of ***The Human Experience.*** It is also an integral part of the "intellectual regeneration" this organization is now determined to create. These facts regarding the sun and its influence on our planet are reproduced because they are a necessary component for sound thinking. We're confident that they will aide us in combating ignorance, and in taking this human race to another level in its relationship with the world and with each other. The following questionnaire and the list of facts that follows this representation is designed to initiate the process.

Questionnaire on the Fundamentals

1- Which is larger the sun or the earth? _____

2- How much larger _____

3- What is the relationship between the 2 bodies?
_____

4- Define Gravity _____

5- The Earth's diameter is _____

6- The earth's circumference is _____

7- The earth's distance from the sun is _____

8- The distance of our orbit around the sun is
_____

9- The speed with which we cover that distance is
_____ miles/hr.

10- The speed of light is _____

11- The speed of sound is _____

FACTS TO LIVE BY

These facts are put together with one purpose only, and that is to combat **Ignorance** and **Powerlessness**, the two deadliest enemies known to mankind. We believe that it is rather unfortunate that facts such as these are only meaningful to a tiny few, the rest prefer to go about their lives enjoying the bliss of ignorance.

1-The first and most fundamental of all these facts is that the Sun is the source of all life on our planet.

2-The second of these is that the sun is 1.300.000 (one million three hundred thousand) time the size of the earth.

3-With its overwhelming superiority in size the sun exerts a gravitational grip over the earth keeping it beaming in its orbit at the speed of 66,000 miles per hour. To compare, the speed of a bullet is 5,600 miles hour.

4-The sun delivers five million (5.000.000) tons of pure energy each second. This energy is equivalent to four hundred million atom bombs, and the frequency is each second.

5-The sun's diameter is calculated at 865,000 miles, the Sun is composed of 80% Hydrogen, 18%Helium, and the remaining 2% is made up of Oxygen, Carbon, Nitrogen, Neon, Iron, Silicon, Magnesium, Sulfur, and other gases.

6-The Sun's circumference is 2.716, 100 miles

7-The Earth's diameter is calculated at 7,973 miles.

8-The Sun's age is estimated at 5.2 billion years.

9-The distance between the earth and the sun is calculated at 93.000.000 miles. *

10-The earth's circumference is 24,902 miles (40,075 km).

11-The speed of light is a constant 186,000 m/sec (300,000 km/sec).

12-The speed of sound is approximately 740 miles per hr. This speed is slightly greater in water, and even more so when traveling through iron.

The writer James Harvey Robinson in his book, *The Mind in The Making* stated:

> I venture to think that if certain seemingly indisputable historical facts were generally known and accepted, and permitted to play a daily part in our thought, the world would forthwith become a very different place from what it now is. We could then neither delude ourselves in the simple-minded way we now do, nor could we take advantage of the primitive ignorance of others. All our discussions of social, industrial, and political reform would be raised to a higher plane of insight and fruitfulness. (p. 6).

Harvey is one of the few modern scholars that celebrated Francis Bacon and his accomplishments as a thinker, writer and intellectual. Bacon is also important because some research reveal that good many of the plays attributed to William Shakespeare were really written by him.

My own inclination towards Harvey Robinson should be obvious, he is one of the few writers that endlessly call for a higher level of thinking among humans, describing with clarity how beneficial this could be to all. This booklet and the organization it speaks for has the same lofty goals.

These facts are fundamental and they constitute a shift in the way we view the world and our place in it. They constitute, if you will, a paradigm shift, and we like to refer to them as the building blocks of human intelligence. To ignore them is to embrace the confusion and hostility that presently defines human relations. They've been in place for billions of years despite our own ignorance of them, the western world became aware of them only a few hundred years ago with the revelation of Giordano Bruno, Nicholas Copernicus and Galileo Galilei. Embracing them changes the conversation entirely, and the subjects we argued over in the past such as: race, religion, social status and others, are no longer as relevant as we made them out to be.   They represent what we like to refer to as the ultimate reality, clearing the mind of superstitions, and made up stories passed on through generations. Only a few short years ago, humans were convinced that they were at the center of the Universe and that the suns, as well as the other celestial bodies, are there for our pleasure and enjoyment.

Advances in science, scientific instrumentation and subsequently the advent of computers, allowed us to discover these as new facts, making them available for those passionate about knowledge and greater understanding. These facts are extremely helpful when practicing reality therapy because it inspires humility.

The speed with which the earth orbits the sun is both fascinating and humbling at the same time.

The total dependency of our earth on the sun and the overwhelming difference in size between the two, reminds even the most ravaged soul of the fact that their fate is equal to that of the six billion other lives on the planet. This new knowledge is empowering, because it liberates the human being from the silly fears of divine punishment or of going to hell. The figures involved in these facts have the potential to shock the senses and to bring us in contact with a new reality, one in which the individual is inspired to do more with his or her lives regardless of their present circumstances. In light of these new facts, all notions of inferiority and superiority disappear almost overnight.

It should be noted that the concept of reality therapy had been utilized for some time prior to this, however the introductions of these facts concerning our immediate and wider environment takes the whole thing to another level. With the mental stimuli that they provide, the individual is now prepared to think at a higher level, to be more creative and to be less of a victim in any situation, in short; to have the power to create their own sense of happiness.

It is humbling to think that were it not for our slow and painful growth through the ages human beings would be no more than a primate living on seeds, roots, fruits and uncooked flesh, wandering unclothed through the woods like a chimpanzee. This humility needs to be preserved if we are to achieve any significant growth as a species. Those struggling with an addiction are beginning to understand this notion, one that reminds them that without humility their chances of overcoming the crippling hold of the drug of choice is next to zero, leaving them at the mercy of an unending cycle of relapse and self-destructive behavior.

The origin and progress of humankind are still misunderstood and misconceived by the overwhelming majority of the population; one would hope that the clarification of these misconception would be high on the list of the educational system. It is imperative that we reconstruct our ideas of humans, and our capacities, freeing ourselves in the process from the persistent misapprehensions that weigh us down. The obstructionists, like the rationalizing theologians, and philosophers are all busy engaged in ratifying existing ignorant mistakes, and discouraging creative thought. In fact, few of us take the pains to study the origins of our cherished convictions; we have a natural repugnance to do so. On the contrary, we prefer to believe what we have been accustomed to accept as true, and when confronted, or when doubt is cast upon any of these assumptions, we seek every manner of excuses for clinging to them.

This proves that our convictions on important matters are not the result of knowledge or critical thought, most of them are pure prejudices in the proper sense of the word. They are not our own ideas, but rather those of others who are no more informed or inspired than ourselves, having inherited them in the same careless and humiliating manner as we. They are; to borrow a quote from Harvey Robinson: ***The whispering of the voices of the herd.***

By studying the manner in which human intelligence appears to have developed, we may eventually understand the perilous quandary in which mankind is now placed, and the way to escape that offers themselves. Ardrey (1972) states:

> We are a transitional species, nature's first, brief, local experiment with self-awareness, a head above the ancestral ape and a head below whatever must come next; we are evolutionary failures, trapped between earth and a glimpse of heaven, prevented by our sure capacity for self-delusion from achieving any triumph more noteworthy that our own sure self-destruction. (p.153).

We appear baffled by the senseless killings of our times while attempting the same old method for dealing with it i.e., the death penalty. But statistics have shown that the threat of the death penalty or its actual exercise, are yet to have an impact on the murder rate that consumes our modern society. We refuse to admit that there might be something in our savage nature that could surface at any time if the conditions are right. It can be triggered by a variety of factors, one of which is power over others, that is, the power to snuff out another life in an instant, in short, to play God. We're all a part of this mass insanity much of which stems from our inability to connect with our savage past. With the sense of power that comes with the weapon the out of control monstrosity we're witnessing at this point in our history should come as no surprise to us.

THE ENLIGHTENMENT ERA

In their book, *Telling the Truth About History,* Joyce Appleby, Lynn Hunt & Margaret Jacob introduce us to history through the prism of science. The first chapter of the book is titled: The Heroic Model of Science, and in it they walk us through the history of science from Copernicus (1473-1543) to the Industrial Revolution with an abundantly clear description of the mindset that accompanied each stage of this development. Their explanations are complex and intellectually challenging but within it we arrive at some truths regarding our present reality and how it came to be. In addition to Copernicus two other scientists played a significant role in breaking the grip the church had on the European society of the time. These were Giordano Bruno (1548-1600) and Galileo Galilei (1564-1642). Copernicus is credited with the heliocentric model for celestial bodies but fear of reprisals from the church prevented him from publishing his findings until he was near the end of his life. Bruno in turn was defiant, not only did he publish findings similar to that of Copernicus but he openly challenged the church, refusing to recant and was burned at the stakes. When Galileo published similar findings, he was denounced, imprisoned and even after recanting forced to spend his remaining years under house arrest. But the Genie was already out of the bottle; scientist and thinkers in Europe and elsewhere had learned of the heliocentric model and were challenging the church's authority on this subject. Many would argue that this sequence of events though spread out over more than a century, marked the beginning of the end for the dark ages. But the enlightenment age did not begin immediately after; strangely enough it was further research on the part of scientists in the protestant world that ushered in the enlightenment. It required thinkers and scientists the likes of Francis Bacon (1561-1626), Rene Descartes (1596-1650), Isaac Newton (1643-1727), Gottfried Leibniz (1646-1716), Emily Du Chatelet (1706-1749), Francois Marie Voltaire (1694-1778), Jean Jacque Rousseau (1712-1778), Denis Diderot (1713-1784), Mary Wollstonecraft (1759-1797), and Immanuel Kant (1724-1804) among others, to really usher in the new era, an era of science and reason. This new era would be marked by experiment, observation, mathematics and new forms of social communication. Established churches and religious dogmas were attacked: "as either deluded or upholders of backward-looking tyrannies, ignorance, prejudice, and superstition."[1] This enlightenment was spread over Western Europe and some parts of the thirteen colonies that were later to make up the United States of America. Appleby, Hunt and Jacob report that one of the founding fathers was also caught up in the frenzy of the enlightenment:" Late in the century Thomas Jefferson expressed faith in the link between science and progress by ordering a composite portrait of the life size bust of Bacon, Locke and Newton."[2] They also paint us a picture of elegant homes of entrepreneurs, merchants and aristocrats of that same period, adorned with miniature planetary systems with movable globes circling the sun in elliptical orbits, made by skilled workers in copper and wood. I have paraphrased here, but the contrast of this image with slaves of the period being indoctrinated with the most repressive brand of Christianity is striking.

---

[1] Appleby, et al. p 33
[2] Appleby, et al. p 25

At the heart of the enlightenment was Newtonian science, and it was also a key component of the Industrial Revolution, but at the height of the celebrations, the authors inform us that: "the same people who taught of themselves as enlightened, as teachers and appliers of Newtonian mechanics were often the profit seeking promoters of steam engines, canal companies, or factory style manufacturing."[3] The leaders of the enlightenment saw science as a means to improving the lives of humans but before long it was limited to serving the interest of greedy industrialists.

In an effort to arrive at the truth about history, science appears to play a unique role. It helps us to understand how we got to this stage in our development. Twisting the truth in this endeavor would defeat the purpose, so in some ironic way we are nudged into honesty. The need to know and understand forces us to tell the story of human development as it really occurred.

A commitment to truth, in the telling of history can carry with it enormous inspirational capabilities. To think that in less than three centuries we went from the dark ages to an enlightenment period is impressive, especially given the fact that this period was followed shortly thereafter by an explosion in technology. Some of this development was detrimental no doubt, but in all, great lessons have been learned. We now discuss facts rather than beliefs, and the wholesale slaughters of the recent past are no longer commonplace. We may teeter on the brink of total annihilation from time to time, but the painful lessons of the past are now burned into the hard drive that makes up our collective desire for self-preservation.

---

[3] Appleby, et al. p 23

Truth in history will remind us of our common ancestry as a specie, and though still resisted in many quarters, this factor is already playing a significant role in the healing process.

LESSONS IN COURAGE
SOCRATES AND GIORDANO BRUNO

In his (1964) publication entitled *Tales of Philosophy*, the Spanish physician Felix Marti Ibanez chronicled the life of some of Europe's most famous philosophers. For their bravery and commitment, we chose Bruno and Socrates as they best illustrate the point we have tried to make throughout this book. Both men paid the ultimate price for defending the truth; they paid with their lives. Socrates because he called on humans to reason and Bruno because he dared to say that the earth was round at a time when all Christians were convinced that it was flat.

SOCRATES

About Socrates, lbañez (1964), tells us that a few thousand years ago, around 350 BC to be exact, a man by the name of Socrates walked the streets of Greece. His most famous quote was "life without philosophy is inconceivable". Socrates was born during the height of the Greek intellectual movement. They questioned everything, including religion and the democratic process, always teaching that truth was never objective or universal, but rather subjective and relative. History's most famous philosopher grew to manhood during Greece's wealthiest period, but he had no interest in riches. Seeing the multitude of articles displayed in the market, he once observed, "How many things there are that 1 do not want". He commonly wore the same rumpled tunic and walked the streets of Athens barefooted. He was trained as a youth in his father's profession of stone carver, won a reputation for bravery and superhuman stamina in the Peloponnesian War. He studied science as a youth, but abandoned it because it seemed a maze of mystery. There was a nobler effort to be made, said Socrates: the study of the mind of man and the quality of his life, thus, as Cicero commented, Socrates brought philosophy down from heaven to earth. Some called him a sophist, but he differed from the sophists by disliking rhetoric and by desiring to strengthen morality instead of weakening it. He consistently avowed that he taught no more than the art of examining ideas when the oracle Delphi was reported to have pronounced him the wisest of men, he protested that he did not possess wisdom but only sought it. Socrates did not preach a return to old dogmatic beliefs but asked such searching questions as: is a natural ethic possible? Can morality be independent of religion? He propounded that men were evil because they were ignorant and thoughtless: if they could see the good, they would choose it; and right thinking would inevitably lead to right conduct. Said he: *Virtue is Knowledge.* If man is the measure of all things, the art of living must begin with the individual and he must question old beliefs, traditions, and creeds, taking nothing for granted in his search for truth. The method of the Socratic dialect was to seek knowledge by question and answer; this probing was intended to expose the shallowness or error of definitions, to expose harmful and false opinions. "Know thyself "was the dictum by which he stung his fellowmen to unflinching self-examination, and when his opponents spoke glibly of such abstractions as courage, fear, honor, he defied them to define their term. He was in high favor as long as Athens was prosperous and powerful, but when that proud city finally fell to Sparta, many leading citizens were scapegoats of the national disgrace and Socrates was no exception. Charges were trumped up that Socrates was setting up gods and corrupting Athenian youth. He was brought to trial found guilty and condemned to end his life by drinking hemlock. To his sorrowing friends he said. "Be of good cheer and say that you are burying my body only". Then he serenely drained the cup of poison that gave him death and immortality. His influence on the development of human thought was enormous, and his emphasis on placing conscience above the law later became a

cardinal tenet of Christianity. His insistence on the clear definition of general concepts, his approach to inductive reasoning, and his faith in an intellectual and moral order remain a
force to this day (p.28). He was the first great European
whose death in 339 BC marks the birth of Europe because he
was the first martyr for European faith. Socrates was the first
European to use intellect as an instrument for obtaining
knowledge of the Universe. In his belief in the divine nature
of the human soul, he was a precursor of Christ. He chose
truth as a guide for humans (p.21). Even with the mind of
Socrates and many others whose stories never really gained
notoriety. Europe continued to grow, albeit ever so slowly.
Italy became the seat of power through Rome and its military
conquests, after all the Roman Empire lasted a thousand
years. But as it shrank in size and in might the Church became
the seat of power and they could command what was left of
the army to do their biddings in drowning the voices of those
who wished to think, to study and to explore. It is in this environment that scientist such as Copernicus, Galileo, and
Giordano Bruno were compelled to do their work. The church
in its backwardness would consider these men to be heretic
and would seek to punish them.

GIORDANO BRUNO

One individual that attempted to shift that paradigm was Giordano Bruno (1548-1600). Bruno was born 5 years after the death of the great Nicolas Copernicus, and he was considered to be a contemporary of Galileo who the story goes was critical of him, but 13 years his junior Bruno had little time for Galileo, he was more concerned with staying alive as his ideas had already enraged the church. The story has it that this Dominican friar born in Italy in 1548 and christened with the name Filippo Bruno was a philosopher, a mathematician, poet and cosmologist, among other things. Bruno's interests in cosmology lead him to support the heliocentric ideas of the Polish astronomer Nicolas Copernicus (1473-1543). At the time, Copernicus was one of the few Europeans to embrace the notion that it is not the Sun that revolves around the Earth, as it was taught by the clergy at the time, but rather the Earth that revolves around this celestial body in its yearly journey. To go against the sacred teachings of the church was considered heresy, and at the time heresy was punishable by death. The power of the clergy instilled fear in Copernicus, and because of that he refused to publish his scientific findings.

History tells us that 21 years after the death of Copernicus one of his most ardent followers namely, Galileo Galilei (1564- 1642) was to come into existence. Free from the fears that paralyzed his hero Nicolas Copernicus, Galileo set out to prove those theories that the earth is not at the center of the world, and that rather than the sun revolving around our planet, it was us that made the yearly journey around the sun. For his boldness and his convic-tion, Galileo paid a heavy price. He was forced to recant and re-nounce his theory, and even after doing so he was placed under house arrest for the remainder of his life.

The dispute between Bruno and Galileo amounted to very lit-tle, they both embraced Copernicus' ideas, and they both suffered for it, what appears to have bothered Galileo about Bruno was his open and confrontational attitude towards the clergy. They were the power, and to confront them spelled death not only for the individual that does so but for anyone else who shares his ideas. Consequently, after they murdered his colleague Bruno, tied at the stakes in living flames, he Galileo bore the brunt of the church's ire, and only a recant of his own ideas could save him from certain death at the hands of the church.

There is no question that the hero of heroes in this story is Giordano Bruno for even though he too recanted a few times, and went in hiding for long periods, he eventually stood to the vicious power of the church that murdered anyone who dared to hold contrary views to theirs.

Ibanez (1964) also wrote extensively about Bruno and in his narrative, he stated that in the XIV century as Europe attempted to shake the yoke of its medieval past, there was an awakening to science and the infinity of space commanded the attention of most thinkers. Among these thinkers there was Nicholas Coper-nicus born in Poland in 1473. His fascination with astronomy had him to construct a crude observatory, and from his findings elab-orated the theory that the earth and all other planets evolved around the sun. Fear of the church's censure made Copernicus delay the publication of his theory until 1543 when he lay dying.

Bruno was born five (5) years after in 1548. He inherited the same interest in astronomy, as did Copernicus. He also studied religion, becoming an outspoken Dominican Friar whose free thinking and fearlessness forced him to flee Venice after charges of heresy were brought against him. Two years later, in Geneva he embraced Calvinism, was imprisoned briefly for publishing an attack on a professor, and after his release taught philosophy at Toulouse. For much of his life Bruno was a lonely wandering philosopher, bombastic, arrogant, with a remarkable ability to outrage authority. He debated with Oxford professors over Copernicus, embraced a pantheistic doctrine that conjoined God and nature as the active and passive element of reality (p.112).

A desire to make peace with the church drew him to Venice, but he was quickly arrested. It was now 1593 and the inquisition was in full swing so they kept him imprisoned for eight years in an attempt to have him change his beliefs. Under questioning, he stated: "I hold the Universe to be infinite, as being the effect of divine power and goodness. Hence, I have declared infinite worlds to exist beside this our earth. It would not be worthy of God to manifest Himself in less than an infinite Universe." Refusing to recant, he told his judges; "You are more afraid of this than I am," and was burned at the stake in1600.

GALILEO GALILEI

Perhaps the saddest of all these stories was that of Galileo Galilei (1564-1642), son of a distinguished philosopher in Roman Italy. Destined at first to become a physician, he became far more interested in Euclid and Archimedes and devoted his time to experiments in physics, including the famous demonstration from the leaning tower of Pisa on the laws of falling bodies. He was the first to build an optic telescope and find, as he said, "with incredible delight" that he could distinguish the mountains on the moon and spots on the sun, discover stars in the Pleiades, observe satellites rotating around Jupiter and obtain glimmering of Saturn and its mysterious rings. His discoveries, which confirmed his belief in the Copernican system, raised a storm of protest: the defenders of the old Ptolemaic system accused the new cosmology of contradicting parts of the Scriptures, and in 1616 the theologians of the Holy Office decreed the heliocentric theory to be heretic. Galileo was warned not to teach the forbidden doctrine, but in 1632 he published his great work in elegant Italian, "Dialogues on the Two Principal Systems of the World" which unflinchingly supported the Copernican system with many of his own observations. He was summoned before the Inquisition in Rome, made to recant, and sentenced to retire in strict seclusion. In 1637 he made his last astronomic discovery, and a few months later became blind. He sadly wrote: "These heavens, this earth, this universe, which by wonderful observation I had enlarged thousand times are henceforth dwindled into the narrow space which I occupy." Galileo died of a fever in1642; the very year Isaac Newton was born (p.lll). The story of the European's quest for knowledge unit the painful birth of western civilization is not at all the history of mankind, because many civilizations preceded theirs and, in most instances,, they were aware that their earth was not the center of the Universe. It took the Europeans several centuries to overcome that thought. In these stalwart bastions of religious darkness, efforts continue to limit human thought and to promote fear and ignorance as a way of life. In order to achieve happiness, you must place yourself above the mundane. You must have the ability of viewing the world and all its nuances from a vantage point that is far above.

ÉMILIE DU CHÂTELET (1706 -1749)

Emilie du Châtelet was a French natural philosopher, mathematician, physicist, and author during the early 1730s until her
untimely death due to childbirth in 1749. du Châtelet's father
Louis-Nicolas, recognizing her early brilliance, arranged for
Fontenelle to visit and talk about astronomy with her when she
was 10 years old Her most recognized achievement is her translation of and commentary on Isaac Newton's book *Principia* con-
taining basic laws of physics. The translation, published posthumously in 1759, is still considered the standard French translation
today. Her commentary includes a profound contribution to Newtonian mechanics—the postulate of an additional conservation
law for total energy, of which kinetic energy of motion is one
element.

Her book entitled th *Foundations of Physics,* circulated
widely, generated heated debates, and was republished and trans-
lated into several other languages within two years of its original
publication. She participated in the famous *vis viva* debate, concerning the best way to measure the force of a body and the best
means of thinking about conservation principles. Posthumously,
her ideas were heavily represented in the most famous text of the
French Enlightenment, the *Encyclopédie* of Denis Diderot and
Jean le Rond D'Alembert, first published shortly after Du Châtelet's death. Numerous biographies, books and plays have been
written about her life and work in the two centuries since her
death. In the early 21st century, her life and ideas have generated
renewed interest.

Du Châtelet's mother, Gabrielle-Anne de Froulay, was brought up in a convent, at the time the predominant educational institution available to French girls and women.[5] While some sources believe her mother did not approve of her intelligent daughter, or of her husband's encouragement of Émilie's intellectual curiosity,[5] there are also other indications that her mother not only approved of Du Châtelet's early education, but actually encouraged her to vigorously question stated fact.[6]

Du Châtelet and Voltaire may have met in her childhood at one of her father's *salons*; Voltaire himself dates their meeting to 1729, when he returned from his exile in London. However, their friendship began in earnest in May 1733, upon her re-entering society after the birth of her third child.

Du Châtelet invited Voltaire to live in her country house at Cirey-sur-Blaise in Haute-Marne, northeastern France, and he became her long-time companion (under the eyes of her tolerant husband). There she studied physics and mathematics and published scientific articles and translations. To judge from Voltaire's letters to friends and their commentaries on each other's work, they lived together with great mutual liking and respect. Sharing a passion for science, Voltaire and Du Châtelet collaborated scientifically. They set up a laboratory in Du Châtelet's home. In a healthy competition, they both entered the 1738 Paris Academy prize contest on the nature of fire, since Du Châtelet disagreed with Voltaire's essay. Although neither of them won, both essays received honorable mention and were published.[12] She thus became the first woman to have a scientific paper published by the Academy.

Her book *Institutions de Physique* ("Lessons in Physics") appeared in 1740; it was presented as a review of new ideas in science and philosophy to be studied by her thirteen-year-old son, but it incorporated and sought to reconcile complex ideas from the leading thinkers of the time. The book and ensuing debate contributed to making her a member of the Academy of Sciences of the Institute of Bologna in 1746.

Du Châtelet's contribution was the hypothesis of the conservation of total energy, as distinct from momentum. Inspired by the theories of Gottfried Leibniz, she repeated and publicized an experiment originally devised by Willem's Gravesande in which balls were dropped from different heights into a sheet of soft clay. Each ball's kinetic energy - as indicated by the quantity of material displaced - was shown to be proportional to the square of the velocity. The deformation of the clay was found to be directly proportional to the height the balls were dropped from, equal to the initial potential energy. Earlier workers, such as Newton and Voltaire, had all believed that "energy" (so far as they understood the concept at all) was indistinct from momentum and therefore proportional to velocity. Energy must always have the same dimensions in any form, which is necessary to be able to relate it in different forms (kinetic, potential, heat...). Newton's work assumed the exact conservation of only mechanical momentum. A broad range of mechanical problems are soluble only if energy conservation is included. The collision and scattering of two point masses is one of them. Leonhard Euler and Joseph-Louis Lagrange established a more formal framework for mechanics using the results from du Chatelet.

She is but one of the many women scientists this species has been fortunate enough to have had over the centuries some equal in brilliance and others whose brilliance may have surpassed hers.

HIDDEN FIGURES

A little over 200 years after Duchatelet death a group of black scientists made history as they played a pivotal role in the North American Program. Haas (2016) reports that as America stood on the brink of a Second World War, there was also a strong appetite for the idea of conquering space. But this appetite could not be satisfied without the calculations and analysis of advanced mathematicians.

Interestingly enough it was women who answered that call as they were recruited by the Langley Memorial Aeronautical Laboratory in 1935 to shoulder the burden of these calculations long before computers or calculators were made available. Even though it was a government program conducting war plans the Langley Memorial Aeronautical Laboratory was a segregated institution so Black scientists and mathematicians were not allowed to participate.

Franklin Delano Roosevelt was president at the time and the civil rights leader A Phillip Randolph approach him with the unfairness of this social reality. Randolph threatened a march on Washington, D.C., to draw attention to these and other forms of racial discrimination. With the threat of 100,000 people swarming to the Capitol, President Franklin D. Roosevelt issued Executive Order 8802, preventing racial discrimination in hiring for federal and war-related work.

At the time, a company called West Computers located in Langley Virginia had been active in conducting the equations that described the functioning of the newly produced airplanes, so when Roosevelt signed his executive order an army of sharp minded Black women were hired by the company to assist in doing the complex calculations that would make these machines safer faster and sleeker. Unrest was brewing in Germany and analysts could tell that another war was afoot that could again require the participation of the United States.

These African American female calculators became a computing pool for specific projects, some like Christine Darden worked to advance supersonic flight, Katherine Johnson calculated the trajectories, launch windows, and emergency back-up return paths for many flights from Project Mercury, including the early NASA missions of John Glenn and Alan Shepard. She was instrumental in the 1969 Apollo 11 flight to the Moon, and was active through the Space Shuttle program.

These black female mathematicians who made the United States space missions possible were referred to as human computers because of the massive figures they were able compute, and because of the complex data they were able to analyze before the advent of computers. Their story is told by Margot Lee Shetterly and played out in a movie by the same name. The book chronicles the lives of Katherine Johnson, Dorothy Vaughan, and Mary Jackson, three mathematicians who overcame discrimination, as women and as African Americans, while working at the National Aeronautics and Space Administration (NASA) during the Space Race. For the first years of their careers, the workplace was segregated and women were definitely kept in the background as Human computers. Their calculations were a determining force in America's greatest achievements in space.

Before John Glenn orbited the earth, or Neil Armstrong walked on the moon, this group of dedicated female mathematicians used pencils, slide rules and adding machines to calculate the numbers that would launch rockets, and astronauts, into space. They were exceptionally talented African American women, some of the brightest minds of their generation. Originally relegated to teaching math in the South's segregated public schools, they were called into service during the labor shortages of World War II, when America's aeronautics industry was in dire need of anyone who had the right stuff.

Suddenly, these overlooked math whizzes had a shot at jobs worthy of their skills, and they answered Uncle Sam's call, moving to Hampton, Virginia and the fascinating, high-energy world of the Langley Memorial Aeronautical Laboratory. Even as Virginia's Jim Crow laws required them to be segregated from their white counterparts, the women of Langley's all-black "West Computing" group helped America achieve one of the things it desired most: a decisive victory over the Soviet Union in the Cold War, and complete domination of the heavens. Starting in World War II and moving through to the Cold War, the Civil Rights Movement and the Space Race, Dorothy Vaughan, Mary Jackson, Katherine Johnson and Christine Darden, participated in some of NASA's greatest successes while they used their intellect to change their own lives, and their country's future.

THE POWER OF WOMEN

After examples like those of Emilie Duchatelet and the sharp minds that made the space program possible, it would not be fair to complete this small pamphlet without an attempt to enhance the value of women, not in the romantic sense as it usually is but as representing more than half of humanity. Instead of regretting the fact that she has never been given the respect and praise she deserves, the language here represents the search for the most effective way for women to begin to exercise their power on this planet. The latent power of women is extraordinary, and it is only a matter of time before that power is demonstrated latent because unless it possesses and believes in the scientific information offered here, it will continue under the psychological influence of a structure invented by men, the very men who have declared her as an inferior being. For reasons that women do not control in almost every country in the world they have fallen into the male version of the creation of this world. Her identity has been defined by the masculine element, and although she recognizes it, it is quite possible that the complexity of the subject still escapes her. Unless women are willing to reject the invented ideas of religion that men have imposed on them over the millennium, any effort to be liberated will be futile.

UNDERSTANDING SEXUALITY

In the glossary of terms Same Sex Attraction was in the introduced as a way of joining the dialogue on the subject related to this naturally occurring phenomenon.

As we speak of the power of knowledge it is imperative that we also include the destructive nature of ignorance. Throughout history little boys and little girls that find themselves attracted naturally to the same sex have been condemned verbally, castigated physically and have been ostracized for something beyond their control. In many areas of the United States; a supposedly developed country; and in many other countries around the world, the ignorance that produces this level of mean-spiritedness goes on unabated.

At the Center for Intellectual Development and its sister organization Club Vizcaya International, it is not the acceptance or rejection of LGBTQ+ community at is discussed but rather the prevailing ignorance of such a large portion of the human family. Rather than discussing the acceptance of someone's nature, our mission is to expose the horrifying nature of the ignorance that allows any human being to be convinced that he or she is superior to another solely because of their sexual nature.

In their suffering, what these young men and women did was reveal to us the massiveness of our own ignorance. It is for that matter that no one holding discriminatory views on another person's sexual nature; will be allowed to operate within either of these organizational structures.

Our mission is to combat ignorance in all of its ugly manifestations, and potential members are welcome into the fold of this organization once they rid themselves of these horrifying and demeaning thoughts.

Part of the reeducation of these potential members includes the understanding that same sex attraction is also a natural occurrence among several other species within the animal kingdom. That said, religious scriptures of any kind are disallowed within this organization, and discussions based on teachings that are born out of ignorance are not accepted. Members are free to practice the religion of their choice, but under no circumstances will the ignorance and prejudices fomented within these religious structures be tolerated here.

ALAN TURING (1912-1954)
THE GAY MAN WHO SAVED THE WORLD

Alan Turing was an English computer scientist, mathematician, logician, cryptanalyst, philosopher and theoretical biologist. He was highly influential in the development of theoretical computer science, providing a formalization of the concepts of algorithm and computation having introduced the world to the Turing machine, at the time a model of a general purpose computer. Turing is widely considered to be the father of theoretical computer science and artificial intelligence. During the Second World War, he worked for the Government Code and Cypher School (GC&CS) at Bletchley Park, Britain's code breaking centre that produced Ultra intelligence. For a time, he led Hut 8, the section which was responsible for German naval cryptanalysis. Here he devised a number of techniques for speeding the breaking of German *ciphers* including improvements to the pre-war Polish *Bombe,* an electromechanical machine that could find settings for the *Enigma* machine. He played a pivotal role in cracking intercepted coded messages that enabled the Allies to defeat the Nazis in many crucial engagements, including the Battle of the Atlantic, and in so doing helped win the war Cooper (2013).

His earlier theoretical concept of a universal Turing machine had been a fundamental influence on the Manchester computer project from the beginning. After Turing's arrival at Manchester, his main contributions to the computer's development were to design an input-output system—using Bletchley Park technology—and to design its programming system. He also wrote the first-ever programming manual, and his programming system

213

was used in the Ferranti Mark I, the first marketable electronic digital computer (1951).

Turing was a founding father of artificial intelligence and of modern cognitive science, and he was a leading early exponent of the hypothesis that the human brain is in large part a digital computing machine. He theorized that the cortex at birth is an "unorganized machine" that through "training" becomes organized "into a universal machine or something like it." Turing proposed what subsequently became known as the Turing test as a criterion for whether an artificial computer is thinking (1950). For his work he elected a fellow of the Royal Society of London in March 1951 one of the highest of honors.

After the war, Turing worked at the National Physical Laboratory, where he designed the ACE, among the first designs for a stored-program computer. In 1948 Turing joined Max Newman's Computing Machine Laboratory at the Victoria University of Manchester, where he helped develop the Manchester computers and became interested in mathematical biology.

Turing was arrested prosecuted in 1952 for homosexual acts, considered criminal in England at the time. He accepted chemical castration treatment, as an alternative to prison but with a criminal record he would never again be allowed to work for Government Communications Headquarters (GCHQ), the British government's postwar code-breaking centre. In the midst of this groundbreaking work, Turing was discovered dead in his bed, poisoned by cyanide. The official verdict was suicide, but no motive was established at the 1954 inquest. His death is often attributed to the hormone "treatment" he received at the hands of the authorities following his trial for being gay. Yet he died more than a year after the hormone doses had ended, and, in any case, the resilient Turing had borne that cruel treatment with what his close friend Peter Hilton called "amused fortitude." Also, to judge by the records of the inquest, no evidence at all was presented to indicate that Turing intended to take his own life, nor that the balance of his mind was disturbed (as the coroner claimed). In fact, his mental state appears to have been unremarkable at the time. Although suicide cannot be ruled out, it is also possible that his death was simply an accident, the result of his inhaling cyanide fumes from an experiment in the tiny laboratory adjoining his bedroom. Nor can murder by the secret services be entirely ruled out, given that Turing knew so much about cryptanalysis at a time when homosexuals were regarded as threats to national security (Copeland 2005).

By the early 21st century Turing's prosecution for being gay had become infamous. In 2009 British Prime Minister Gordon Brown, speaking on behalf of the British government, publicly apologized for Turing's "utterly unfair" treatment. Four years later Queen Elizabeth II granted Turing a royal pardon. (Copeland 2005).

OTTO RANK (1884-1939)

Born in Vienna Austria in 1884, Rank: was 28 years Freud's junior, and what is interesting in this relationship is that Rank looked up to Freud as his adopted father. He was Freud closest disciple and colleague from 1906 through 1926, the formative years of psychoanalytic movement. Freud valued his expertise in art, music, literature, anthropology, history, science, and philosophy. Freud advised him not to go to medical school, but to complete his academic education. Rank obliged and obtained his PhD at age 28 at the University of Vienna in 1912. Freud, only 5.7" tall would affectionately refer to Rank, 5.3" as "Little Rank" in his letters to another of his closest colleagues, Carl Jung who stood above them both at 6 feet tall. In 1935 after a lifetime as Freud's protégé and follower, Rank left Europe and took up residence in the United States. He was already becoming disenchanted with the movement, criticizing it at being stagnated, and excessive in its attempts to psycho-analyze everything almost to an extreme. Becker (1972) offers us one of Otto Rank's most famous quotation uttered as he was beginning the process of breaking away from Freud and psychoanalysis:

Suddenly....while I was resting in bed it occurred   to me what really was (or is) Beyond Psychology. You know what? Stupidity! All that complicated and elaborate explanation of human behavior is nothing but an attempt to give a meaning to one of the most powerful motives of behavior namely, Stupidity.! I began to think that is even more powerful than badness, meanness—because many actions or reactions that appear mean are simply stupid and even calling them bad is a justification (p 251).

The relationship between Freud and Rank lasted 20 years and the two men; it is fair to say; became a lot better as a result of it, despite the difference in age. It is also interesting to know that they both died in 1939. Freud on September 23rd and Rank on October 31st of that year.

ERIC FROMM (1906-1980)

Eric Fromm was perhaps the greatest and most faithful of Freud's followers. A prolific writer himself, Fromm dedicated much of his life and energy giving the world a greater understanding of Freud, his times, his personality, and his work. Nowhere is this done more effectively than in his book, *Sigmund Freud's Mission*. Here Fromm gives us a personal look at Freud and all that is connected to him. He was Freud's junior by 44 years, but Fromm did more detailed and honest study about Freud than any single individual. As his biography suggests, Fromm's theory is a rather unique blend of Freud and Marx. Freud of course, emphasizes the unconscious, biological drives, repression, and so on. In other words, Freud postulated that our characters are determined by biology Marx on the other hand saw people as determined by their society and most especially by their economic systems. He added to this mix of two deterministic systems, something quite foreign to them: The idea of freedom. He allows people to transcend the determinisms that Freud and Marx attribute to them. In fact, Fromm makes freedom the central characteristic of human nature. There are; Fromm points out; examples where determinism alone operates. A good example of nearly pure biological determinism a la Freud is animals (at least simple ones). Animals don't worry about freedom their instincts take care of everything. Woodchucks, for example don't need career counseling to decide what they're going to be when they grow up; they are going to be woodchucks! Two events shaped Fromm's life, and these two took place long before he met Freud. The first at age 12 had to do with a female friend of the family around 25 years of age. As he described it: She was beautiful, attractive and in addition a painter, the first painter I ever knew he stated. I remember having heard that she had been engaged, but after some time had broken the engagement; I remember that she was almost invariably in the company of her widowed father. As I remember him, he was an old uninteresting and rather unattractive man or so I thought (perhaps my judgment was somewhat biased by jealousy). Then one day I heard the shocking news; her father had died, and immediately afterwards, she had killed herself and left a will that stipulated that she wanted to be buried with her father. This news hit the 12-year-old Eric very hard and he found himself asking many questions, some of which he found answers to later on in his life in Freud. The second event took place two years after with World War I. At the tender age of 14 he saw the extremes that Nationalism could go to. All around him he heard the message: We Germans (or more precisely Christian Germans) are great; they, the English and their allies are cheap mercenaries. The hatred, the war hysteria, frightened him. So again, he wanted to understand something irrational the irrationality of mass behavior, and he found some answers, this time in the writings of Karl Marx. At age 22 Fromm had already received his Ph.D. in Psychology, but the uniqueness of his contribution to psychoanalysis was his own emphasis on Love and Rationale. He argued that the highest value for any human being consisted in finding unity with the world through full development of specifically human capacities of

Love and Reason. All the intellect in the world could not replace the value of love and reason. Fromm was baffled by the many trends he observed as a scholar and researcher. He described himself as a Radical Humanist and described radical humanism as the philosophy that emphasizes the oneness of the human race, the capacity of each individual to develop his or her own powers and to arrive at inner harmony while helping to establish a peaceful world.

CARL JUNG (1875-1961)

Perhaps the most controversial of all of Freud's relation-
ships is the one he maintained with Carl Jung. Like Rank and
all the other followers, Carl Gustav Jung, got to know Freud
through his writings since he was a prolific writer and wrote
on a variety of subjects. He admired Freud and got a chance
to meet him in Vienna in 1907. The story goes that after they
met, Freud cancelled all his appointments for the day, and
they talked for 13 hours straight, such was the impact of the
meeting of these two great minds. Freud eventually came to
see Jung as the crown prince of psychoanalysis and his heir
apparent, but Jung had been entirely sold on Freud's theory
and their relationship began to cool in 1909 during a trip to
America. They were entertaining by analyzing each other's
dreams, when Freud began to an excess of resistance to
Jung's effort at analysis. Freud finally said they'd have to
stop because he was afraid he would lose his authority. Jung
felt rather insulted. The following account from Eric Fromm
in his book Sigmund Freud Mission tells more about the relationship and gives further insight into Freud the man.
Freud's dependency on the mother figure was not restricted
to his wife and his mother. It was transferred to men, older
ones like Breuer, contemporaries like Fliess and pupils like
Jung. But Freud had a fierce pride in his independence and a
violent aversion to being the protégée. This pride made him
the awareness of dependency and negated it completely by
breaking off the friendship when the friend failed in the com-

plete fulfillment of the motherly love. Thus, his great friendships follow the same rhythm, intense friendship for several years, then complete break, usually to the point of hatred. This was the fate of his friendship With Breuer, Fleiss, Jung, Adler, Rank and even Ferenczi, the loyal pupil who never dreamed of separating himself from Freud and his movement. Breuer, an older and successful colleague, had given Freud the seed of the idea, which was to develop into psychoanalysis. Breuer had been treating a patient, Ana O., and discovered that whenever he put her into hypnosis and made her tell him what was bothering her, she would feel relieved of her symptoms (depression and confusion).Breuer understood that the symptoms were caused by an emotional upheaval she had experienced while nursing her sick father, and furthermore he understood that the irrational symptoms were meaningful once one understood their origins. Thus, Breuer gave Freud the most important suggestion he ever received in his life, a suggestion which formed the basis of the central idea of psychoanalysis. Beyond that, Breuer acted toward Freud as a fatherly friend, including also considerable material help. How did this relationship end? True, there was a developing theoretical disagreement, because Breuer did not follow Freud in all this theory about sex. But certainly, such theoretical disagreement would not normally lead to a personal break, not to speak of the hatred Freud felt toward his former friend and benefactor. Or to put it in Jones' words: The scientific difference alone could not account for the bitterness with which Freud wrote about Breuer in his correspondence with Fleiss during the 1890s.

One valid criticism of Sigmund Freud is that he failed to describe anything positive about the unconscious. He strongly believed that the goal of psychotherapy was to reveal thoughts hidden in the unconscious or subconscious, but he made it sound so unpleasant that one had to think twice whether the efforts to go there were really worth it. He described it as a cauldron of seething desires, a bottomless pit of perverse and incestuous cravings, a virtual burial ground for frightening experiences which persistently came back to haunt us. Not exactly the kind of thing anyone looks forward to bringing into consciousness. In his earlier years Freud speaks of the oedipal complex and out of intellectual laziness many of the neo-Freudians find it difficult to transcend that narrow characterization of Him.

ROLLO MAY (1909 - 1994)

The circle of men responsible for what is loosely known as the Psychoanalysis Movement is completed with Rollo. He was the only American in that circle that lived to the ripe old age of 83, but his upbringing was less than pleasant, with parents divorcing when he was still a child and his sister suffered from severe psychosis. To make matters worse, May also had a serious bout with tuberculosis around the age of 30 that almost cost him his life. He spent three years in a sanatorium and while contemplating the possibilities of death, he threw himself into reading. The existentialist writings of Soren Kierkegaard became one of his favorite subjects. At the White Institute he met and became acquainted with Eric Fromm. Earlier on, upon graduation from College, he spent some time in Europe where he met, became acquainted with and was inspired by Alfred Adler. In 1953 May published his work entitled "Man's search for Himself". In it he offers some deep and accurate analysis into the psyche of modern man and his afflictions. The very preface of the book is vintage May: One of the blessings of living in an age of anxiety is that we are forced to become aware of ourselves. The painful insecurity on all sides gives us new incentive to ask, is there perhaps some important source of guidance and strength we have overlooked? People ask rather, how can one attain inner integration in such a disintegrated world? Or they question: How can anyone undertake the long development toward self-realization in a time when practically nothing is certain either in the present or in the future? Most thoughtful people have pondered these questions. The psychotherapists have no magic answers. But there is something in addition to his technical training and his own self-understanding which gives an author the courage to rush in where angels fear to tread, thus offering his ideas and experience on these difficult questions. This something is the wisdom the psychotherapist gains in working with people who are striving to overcome their problems. He has the extraordinary, if often taxing, privilege of accompanying persons through their intimate and profound struggles to gain new integration. And dull indeed would be the therapists who did not get glimpses into what blinds people from themselves, and what block them in finding values and goals they can affirm. I do not see how the therapist can be anything but deeply grateful for what he is taught daily about the issues and dignity of life by those who are called his patients. Our aim is to discover ways in which we can stand against the insecurity of our times, to find center of strength within ourselves, and as far as we can to point the way towards achieving values and goals which can be depended upon in a day when very little is secure. One of the first things necessary for a creative relationship with others is to remove the subject of religious from the dialogue. He feels that making god an entity, a being over other beings, located in space is a carryover from a primitive view, full of contradictions and easily refutable. Religion or lack of it is shown not to some intellectual or verbal formulation but to one's total orientation to life. Religion is whatever the individual takes it to be. One's religious attitude is to be found at that point where he has a conviction that there are values in human existence worth living and dying for. The point we wish to emphasize is that psychologically religion is to be understood as a way of relating to one's existence.

These six giants of the field of psychology are presented to help familiarize students with the pioneers of the field. In keeping up with its commitment to bringing more students into the field of psychology, particularly at Saybrook University where I am putting the finishing touches on my own PhD, it seems natural to offer them a synopsis of the views of these great thinkers as they endeavor to take the field to higher heights and making it a more effective part of the life of those in need of assistance.

AN ENCOURAGING OUTLOOK

If the species is to advance, intellect will have to play a greater role than it does today. Much has been said about the fan cy gadgets children are exposed to today and their extraordinary abilities to master these gadgets in zero time, but some doubts remain as to whether this has had much effect on the intellectual growth of these children, and their sense of independence as individuals. Although there are hardly any signs of organized resistance on the horizon, it is hard to imagine the species holding steadfast to these discredited belief systems for much longer, but highlighting the damage they continue to cause on young minds appears to be perhaps the one inevitable way of confronting a structure that has been so effective in slowing human growth and bringing so much misery to so many over the ages.

As we embark on this quest to understand human behavior, particularly as it is affected by belief or belief systems, it is important to recognize that for reasons beyond our explanation, there is precious little data available on this subject. One gets the impression that the power to ostracize those who dare to openly criticize the phenomenon of belief remains an ever-present deterrent for scholars who by their own nature have resisted the power and control held by religions of all sway even in our era of modernity. The data available on belief and its effect on human behavior, particularly its effects on human brutality is scant, a factor that causes this research to be all the more challenging, for despite its importance and the enormous effect belief has had on the human psyche, as well as on human behavior, scholars everywhere have avoided this issue at all cost. This seemingly collective decision; at least at a subconscious level; has had the effect of leaving the masses in every culture and in every society, up to their own devices. Since the brightest among them avoid the subject, they are left to figure out this subject on their own despite the confusing quandary in which nearly all happens to find themselves in, particularly as it relates to this subject.

It is interesting that Harris *et al* (2009) would argue that the industrial world anticipated the demise of religion as we know it given the extraordinary promises of technology and a more advance way of thinking as it was expected. For reasons that are nearly impossible to explain, this turned out not to be the case. This prompt the researchers to delve into the phenomenon of belief and the mechanisms involved in the stranglehold it has succeeded in maintaining over nearly all of those who refer to themselves as humans. According to Harris *et al* (2009) there appears to be a continuous correlation between culture and religion although the authors fail to give us any definition for either of those terms. It behooves us then to pause and attempt to identify these terms before we advance in this discussion thus I shall refer to religion as the process through which human beings attempt to identify with the forces responsible for their existence, and for that same purpose I shall define culture as "learned behavior." As we proceed with these simple definitions, we recognize that the guess work has been taken out of the subject.

Norman et al (2008) tells us that the human mind possesses a limited capacity for processing information, and it may be fair to say that this may just be the central point of why dogma and belief in the hands of skillful manipulators, have been able to maintain such grasp on humans everywhere. The question to be asked is, at what point do we allow irrationality to govern the affairs of humans? In describing the general penchant for fiction that appears to run common in all humans Norman et al (2008) explains that we embrace only a portion of the information that is fed to us by way of fiction, that even though at first, we appear to believe it all, as some degree of rationality imposes itself we begin to drop some of what is just too obviously ludicrous.

In addition to the young men and women struggling to overcome the tyranny of their parents' religion, the group we seek to involve in this movement are women willing to take the extra step in ridding themselves of all vestiges of male dominance, psychologically and physically. These are the ultimate heroes, and the ones we celebrate above all else. With their work and commitment, the respect and adoration for women can be restored.

CLUB VIZCAYA INTERNATIONAL

It is at this point in the writing that we must warn you that the Center for Intellectual Development is not just a gloom and doom organization taking on the evils of society; on the contrary, it is a fun filled organization committed to the health and happiness of its members. Teaming up with Club Vizcaya International an organization managed by my wife Yolanda, clients receive a taste of both worlds. In one they grow intellectually, become fortified emotionally, and learn the reality about the world. In the other they are set a loose to carry on and have fun in healthy environment. She organizes the parties in which members of both the club and the organization are pampered and catered to as they make claim of their right to happiness. Healthy eating and moderate drinking are encouraged at these fun-filled activities, and members come away with the notion that the world is theirs for the taking. A unique building program has members visualizing the possibilities of owning their homes outright, not in partnership with any bank or manipulating financial institution. An intense *Cardiosalsa* and a unique approach to cooking and dining keeps members healthy and happy as they in turn work to improve the lives of others. This is what we refer to as a win situation.

Vizcaya communities is the upscale housing program championed by Club Vizcaya International, and it rounds out the actual intentions of this movement which is to improve people's life by reducing for them the cost of living. That of course, is only for members, and membership is available to everyone providing they're able to follow some basic behavior rules.

The open-air concerts and other events planned by Club Vizcaya International are labeled: ***Celebrating Humanity***. Most if not all of them will be fundraisers for targeted causes, and chief among those causes is child illness. Members of our organization are committed to frequent visits to children's hospital to bring joy where they can and to remain grounded as it relates to their own good fortune.

CARDIOSALSA

If we pretend to improve the lives of those who choose to be part of this process it is necessary to start with health, it does not serve us if the health of all those operating in this organization have their health compromised. Both the Center for Intellectual Development and Club Vizcaya International are committed to the health of all those who operate within their ranks, and for this we have developed an extensive health program that begins first with adequate information on everything the individual is required to do in order to preserve his or her health.

As an effective support network, we recognize how difficult it is for the individual to remain motivated to take and maintain all the actions needed to remain healthy. That is why we take persuasiveness and emotional support seriously, seeing it as crucial elements in achieving the goals the individual sets out for him or herself. Health experts working in this organization will ensure that every member receives the assistance needed to Achieve their goals.

To maintain the health of all, physicians recommend that the individual keeps moving and that, we recognize, requires a certain degree of motivation. One of the most effective ways to keep moving is through dance and where dance is concerned there are few that meet that purpose better than the dance form we've come to know as *salsa*. It is a way of dancing that gives instant happiness to its practitioners, and that allows them to practice it more frequently and for more extended periods, providing the environment is healthy. The events at Club Vizcaya International fulfill these goals, as they provide members with a safe environment, and offer them the opportunity to exercise for extended hours in accordance with the recommendations of their physician, health fitness consultants and their nutritionist.

Our own nutritional programs provide members with the most advanced information on the methods that exist for the maintenance of health. Members receive information on free radicals, on antioxidants, on hydrogenation of fats, on the abuse of refined carbohydrates, infections, inflammations and on cell deterioration.

The cost of participation in an advanced program like ours is affordable to everyone so we invite you to participate.

CONCLUSION

There is not much that can be said by way of conclusion on a subject as complex as the one dealt with here, so at the risk of boring the reader I will attempt to end on a high and hopefully more encouraging note.

Strange as it may sound, what is proposed on these pages is a new approach to psychology, the psychotherapeutic process, and to human relation in general. How far this proposed new approach reaches in anyone's guess but I have committed the remainder of my time on this planet to see to it that this proposal takes root, and that those who wish to benefit from this new approach can do so without reservations or limitations. Fortunately, it does not require a new structure, it simply builds on what is already in existence, adding a twist to it. That twist is brutal honesty regarding not just the birth of our planet, but also the beginning of life on it and everything that was to come thereafter. As simplistic as this may appear, those capable of handling this approach are few, and they are far in between. That said, the process is already on its way, and all of it is being shouldered by the Center for Intellectual Development, the organization I happen to be heading. The name was chosen in order that there be no doubt whatsoever regarding what the organization stands for.

The vigorous application of the intellect is a practice that is greatly discouraged in our world, and there are those who believe that this is by design. I have no opinion on whether this is meant to be, I know however, that for one to participate within these ranks they must be willing to apply the intellect.

This is also not an attempt to separate thinkers from non-thinkers but rather a determination to exclude those who have given up their rights to think and to function at a higher level intellectually.

The organization is unconcerned with numbers or statistics, all that it concerns itself with is that those who choose to function at a higher level find a place that encourages such determination, and that they succeed in their goal to make this a better species.

Understanding the trajectory of the human species is a key component of emotional stability and mental health. That is the premise behind the psychotherapeutic method introduced in these pages.

Bibliografía

Ardrey, R. (1963). *Génesis Africano: Una investigación personal en los orígenes animales y la naturaleza de la humanidad.* Nueva York N.Y. Delta Books.

Borden, W. (1999). *Enfoques comparativos en psicoterapia dinámica.* Binghamton N.Y. Haworth Press.

Bradley, K., y Cartledge, P. (2011). La historia mundial de la esclavitud: Volumen 1. Nueva York NY: Universidad de Cambridge Press.

Breuer, J. Freud, S, y Luckhurst, N. (2004). Estudios en histeria. Nueva York. Penguin Books.

Bringuier, J.C., & Piaget, J. (1977). Conversaciones con Jean Piaget. Francia Ediciones Laffont, S.A.

Brodie, F. (1971). Nadie conoce mi historia: La vida de José Smith, el profeta Mormón. New York N.Y. Alfred A. Knopf Publishers.

Brodrick, A. (1964). Man and his ancestry. New York. N Y. Fawcett World Library.

Brown, P. (2010). Iglesia de mentiras. San Francisco, CA. Jossey-Bass.

Carlisle, R. (1975). *Las raíces del nacionalismo negro.* Port Washington NY: National University Press.

Carter, R. (1999). *Mapeando la Mente.* Berkeley y Los Ángeles. Universidad de California Press.

Colaiaco, J. (2006). Frederick Douglass y el Cuatro de Julio. Nueva York NY: Palgrave Macmillan.

deMause, L.(1974). La historia de la infancia. Nueva York, N.Y. La Psicohistoria Press.

deMause, Lloyd. (1992). La historia del abuso infantil. El Diario de la Psicohistoria, 25. (3).

de Mause, Lloyd. (2002). La Vida Emocional de las Naciones. Nueva York. Otros Press LLC.

Despert, L. (1970). El niño emocionalmente perturbado:

una investigación en patrones familiares. Garden City,
N.Y. Double Day & Company, Inc.

Dewey, J. (1902). La escuela y la sociedad. Chicago IL La
Prensa de la Universidad de Chicago.

Dodds, A. (2009). Las fes Abrahámicas Continuidad y
discontinuidad en la doctrina cristiana e islámica. *Evangelical Quarterly, 81 (3), pp 24, 230, 253.*

Duncan, B. Miller, S, y Sparks, J. (2004). El cliente heroi
co, Una manera revolucionaria de mejorar la efectividad
a través de la terapia dirigida a los clientes, informada
por los resultados. San Francisco, CA. Jossey-Bass, Editores.

Ellis, A. & Dryden, W. (1997). La práctica de la terapia
racional de la conducta emotiva. New York Springer
Publishing Co.

Erikson, E. (1980). Identidad y ciclo de vida, Volumen 1.
New York W.W. Norton & Company, Inc.

Gates, H. L. (1994). Autobiografías de Frederick Dou
glass. Nueva York NY: Clásicos literarios de los Estados Unidos.

Genovese, E. (1972). El mundo que los esclavos hicieron.
Nueva York, NY: Random House Inc.

Green, D. (1998). Vidas ocultas: voces de niños en Améri
ca Latina y el Caribe. Londres. Cassell Wellington
House.

Harlan, L. (1983). Booker T. Washington: El mago de
Tuskegee. Nueva York. NY: Oxford University Press.

Harris, S. (2005). El fin de la fe: la religión, el terror y el

futuro de la razón. Nueva York N.Y. W. W. Norton &
Company.

Haugen, B. (2006). Joseph Stalin: Dictador de la Unión
Soviética. Minneapolis MN. Compass Point Books.

Ibáñez, F. (1964). Tales of Philosophy. New York N Y. Clark son N Potter, Inc/Publisher.

Kramer, R. (1976). Maria Montessori: una biografía. Chi cago Ill. Universidad de Chicago Press.

Levering, D. (2000). W.E.B Du Bois, la lucha por la igual dad y el siglo Americano, 1919-1963. New York, NY: Henry Holt y Company, LLC.

Lloyd, P. y Fernyhough, C. (1999). Lev Vygotsky: evalua ciones críticas, Volumen 1. Nueva York Rutledge.

Loentz, Elizabeth. (2007). Permítanme continuar diciendo la verdad: Bertha Pappenheim como autora y activista. Jerusalem Hebrew Union College Press.

MacMillan, Margaret. Juegos Peligrosos, Usos y Abusos de la Historia. The Modern Library Books, una división de Random House Nueva York, 2008.

Manning, S. (2004). Psicología, simbolismo y saber: en frentar la disfunción religiosa en un mundo cambiante. Otsego MI: Page Free Publishing, Inc.

Mc Ginn, L. (1997). Revista Americana de Psicoterapia. 51 (3), p. 309.

Miller, A. (1998). Las consecuencias políticas del maltrato infantil. El Diario de la Psicohistoria, 26. (2).

Miller, W.R. y Rollnick, S. (1987). Entrevista motivacio nal: preparando al individuo para el cambio.

Miller, W. R. (1994). Manual de terapia de realce motiva cional: una guía de investigación clínica para terapeutas que tratan a personas con abuso y dependencia de al- cohol Volumen 20.

Montessori, M. & Wyman, H. (1912). El Método Montes sori: La pedagogía científica aplicada a los niños en la educación. Nueva York Frederick A. Stokes Co.

Montessori, M. (2004). El Descubrimiento del Niño. Delhi, India. Aakar Books.

Mooney, C.G. (2000). Teorías de la infancia. Introducción a Dewey, Montessori.

Moore, J. (1965). Booker T. Washington, W.E.B. Du Bois, y la lucha por el levantamiento racial. Wilmington, DE. Scholarly Resources Inc.

Payne, G.H., & Jacobi, A. (1916). El niño en el progreso humano. Nueva York. Hijos de G. P. Putnam.

Poussant, A. (2000). *Lay My Burden Down: El suicidio y la crisis de salud mental entre los Afroamericanos*. Boston MA. Beacon Press.

Woodson, C.G. (1933). La educación errónea del Negro. Washington, DC: The Associate Publishers Inc.

Reuter, C. (2004). Mi vida es un arma: La historia del bombardeo suicida. Princeton N.J Princeton University Press.

Riak, J. (2009). Plain Talk About Spanking. Disponible [Enlínea] http://www.nospank.net/pt2009.htm.

Rieber, R. y Robinson, D. (2001). Wilhelm Wundt En la historia: la creación de una psicología científica. Nueva York Plenum Publishers.

Robinson, B.A. (2004). Consultores de Ontario sobre la tolerancia religiosa Obtenido 1/11/11 http://www.religioustolerance.org/flds.htm

Roekeach, M. (1960). Entendiendo los valores humanos: individuales y societales. Nueva York, Nueva York: The Free Press.

Strauss, M. Donnelly, D. (2009). *Azotando al diablo que llevan por dentro: el castigo corporal en las familias estadounidenses y sus efectos sobre los niños*. Nuevo Brunswick. Editores Transaccionales.

Strauss, M. (2009). Universidad de New Hampshire Los

niños que son azotados tienen coeficientes de inteligencia más bajos, hallazgos de investigación nuevos. *Ciencia diaria*. Disponible (En línea) http: /www.sciencedaily.com

Declaración de las Naciones Unidas de los Derechos del Niño. Disponible [En línea.] www2.ohchr.org/English/law/crc.htm.

Verhellen, E. (1996). Monitorización de los derechos del niño. La Haya, Países Bajos. Kluwer Law International.

Wall, E. &, Pulitzer, L. (2009). Inocencia robada: Creciendo en una secta polígama, y liberándome de Warren Jeffs. New York, N.Y., Harper Collins.

Wampold, B. E. (2001). El gran debate de la psicoterapia: modelos, métodos y hallazgos. Mahwah N. J. Lawrence Earlbaum Associates Publishers.

Williams, E. (1944). Capitalismo y esclavitud Chapel Hill, NC: La Universidad de Carolina del Norte.

Williams, C. (1987). La destrucción de la civilización Negra, Grandes logros de una raza 4.500 A.C. a 2000 A.D. Chicago IL: Third World Press.

Woodson, C. (1933). La educación errónea del Negro. San Diego, CA: Los editores del árbol del libro.

Wundt, W. M. (1904). Principios de psicología fisiológica, Volumen 1. Nueva York. El Macmillan Co.

Gilligan, C. (1982). *In A Different Voice*, Cambridge MA: Harvard University Press.

www.ingramcontent.com/pod-product-compliance
Lightning Source LLC
Chambersburg PA
CBHW030836300326
41935CB00036B/176